A HOUSE DIVIDED

A House Divided

SUSPICIONS OF MOTHER-DAUGHTER INCEST

[Based on a true story]

Paul R. Abramson, Ph.D.
Department of Psychology
University of California, Los Angeles

Steven D. Pinkerton, Ph.D.
Department of Psychiatry and
Behavioral Medicine
Medical College of Wisconsin

W·W·NORTON

NEW YORK · LONDON

The text of this book is composed in Sabon
with the display set in Meta
Composition by PennSet, Inc.
Manufacturing by The Courier Companies, Inc.
Book design by M Space

Library of Congress Cataloging-in-Publication Data
Abramson, Paul R.
    A house divided : suspicions of mother-daughter incest (based
on a true story) / Paul R. Abramson and Steven D. Pinkerton.
        p. cm.
    Includes bibliographical references.
    ISBN 0-393-97635-1 (pbk.)
    1. Incest—California—Mendocino. 2. Child sexual abuse—
California—Mendocino. 3. Mothers and daughters—California—
Mendocino. I. Pinkerton, Steven D. II. Title.

HV6570.8.C2 A27 2000
364.15¢36—dc21   00-033224

W.W. Norton & Company, Inc., 500 Fifth Avenue, New York,
N.Y. 10110
www.wwnorton.com

W. W. Norton & Company Ltd., 10 Coptic Street, London WC1A
1PU
1 2 3 4 5 6 7 8 9 0

Paul Abramson: To my mentors and prophets: Paul Wohlford, Phil Goldberg, Don Mosher, Ruth Fisher, Evie McClintock, and Keith Witt.

Steven Pinkerton: Dedicated with love to my Nonnie (Christine Koehn) and to the memory of my grandparents: Edward Koehn, Lola Pinkerton, and Dale Pinkerton.

PREFACE

A House Divided tells the emotionally harrowing tale of a mother's fight to retain custody of her daughter amid horrifying accusations of mother-daughter incest. Several years ago, Helen Cross, a young, single mother in Mendocino, California, was accused of an unforgivable crime: sexually abusing her five-year-old daughter. Charged with incest and threatened with losing her daughter for good, she turned to me (Dr. Paul Abramson) for assistance in preparing her defense. As a professor of psychology and a recognized authority on childhood sexual abuse, I thought I could help. This is the true story of my involvement in the Cross case and its many twists and turns.

Helen was a bright young woman, a successful single mom, and a sexual adventurer with a checkered past. But was she also a child abuser? As the reader will discover, Helen's case unfolds as a psychological suspense story, with an extraordinary cast of characters. *A House Divided* combines interviews, trial transcripts, police reports, and other documentary sources to recount this intriguing tale. (To preserve anonymity, names, locations, occupations, and minor plot details have been altered. Also, portions of the narrative and trial dialogue have been modified to enhance readability.)

This unusual case provides an ideal springboard for a serious consideration of the legal and psychological issues underlying the assessment and prosecution of mother-daughter incest. What should the standard of evidence be in such cases? And what role should the rarity of mother-daughter incest play in determining whether a case is brought to trial?

Commentary on these issues and other relevant questions is woven throughout the story presented here. A technical exploration of these topics, and on the limits of rational thinking in emotionally charged cases such as mother-daughter incest, is reserved for the epilogue.

ACKNOWLEDGMENTS

The authors would like to thank Emily Steele for transcribing and typing the courtroom scenes; Allan Hauth and Mary Turk for providing bibliographic assistance; and Ralph Resenhoeft for his tireless dedication. We especially appreciate the suggestions of our friends, family, and colleagues who were kind enough to read through preliminary drafts of the manuscript: Keith Abramson, Robert Galler, Gina Hendrickson, David McDermott, Georgia McDermott, Judy Pinkerton, Jamie Forrest Raney, Don Symons, and Keith Witt fall into this category, as does our editor at W. W. Norton, Jon Durbin.

A House Divided

AN UNUSUAL REQUEST

I had just arrived in my office in the psychology department at UCLA and was peacefully munching on a breakfast bagel, scattering crumbs on a scientific manuscript I was writing, when the phone began to ring. After taking a moment to curse the interruption, I picked up the receiver.

The woman on the other end of the line introduced herself as Helen Cross. She explained that she had gotten my name from Dr. Maggie Schultz, who is a professor of clinical psychology at UC Berkeley. Helen said that Dr. Schultz had recommended me highly, based on my reputation as a human sexuality researcher and my many years of experience serving as an expert witness in sexual abuse, pornography, and other sex-related cases.

"I'm going to court in a couple months and I'm afraid they're going to take away my little girl, Katie—this time for good," Helen began in a soulless monotone that betrayed the emotional significance of her words.

"It started a few months ago. They—Child Protective Services—came and took her away. I didn't get her back for six days. They were the worst days of my life, and they were horrible for Katie too. Now she feels guilty, like it was all her fault. But really it was just a misunderstanding.

What happened was that Katie had been sexually acting out at school and they reported it. Then, when the social workers came to investigate, they thought Katie was sexually precocious—because she knew correct anatomical terms—and took that as evidence that she was overly sexualized. And then they misinterpreted something Katie said and decided to take her away from me. I got her back, but now there's this court case and I really need your help."

Helen paused briefly to catch her breath. When she resumed, I could tell by the rising pitch of her voice that she had finally come to the crux of the matter. "They want to take my daughter away, because . . . Because they think I sexually molested her!"

After dropping this little bombshell, Helen remained silent for several seconds. Finally, she said, "Dr. Abramson, I love my daughter more than anything and I would never hurt her. I know you're an expert in these cases. If you'll help me, I'm sure we could get them to drop the charges."

However, as Helen laid out the circumstances surrounding her case in greater detail, two things became clear. First, Helen was being unduly optimistic. Yes, there was a possibility that the charges would be dropped, but it looked serious to me. Most likely, she would lose her child and, possibly, go to jail.

But maybe I could help. I told her that I would see what I could do, and arranged to meet her in person as soon as possible.

Although I have given expert testimony in scores of sexuality cases, I have always put my scientific research first. During my twenty-four years as a professor of psychology at UCLA, I have published articles on such diverse topics as masturbation, the menstrual cycle, and scientific methods for assessing the impact of AIDS prevention strategies. I have also written several books and edited several more.

Though focusing on sex sounds exciting, in actuality, sex research is often dry and technical. Much of the work that I've done has been highly theoretical—more equations than erections. Once in a while, though, a case like Helen's comes along that combines the potential to investigate a rare and intriguing phenomenon (allegations of mother-daughter incest).

The few cases of mother-daughter incest that have been reported in the clinical literature typically involve mentally imbalanced mothers. Thus, if Helen was lying, I would gain access to a unique clinical case. On the other hand, if Helen was telling the truth, I could help avert a painful miscarriage of justice. But before I could help her, I needed to find out whether or not she was telling the truth.

THE ARREST

Helen, who lived in Mendocino, a small town in northern California, flew to L.A. on Saturday and met me at UCLA to discuss the case further. When I greeted her at my office door, I was immediately stuck by her strawberry blond hair and deep green eyes. She was an attractive woman in her early forties, about 5´6˝ with "weight appropriate to height," as the personal ads say.

Not surprisingly, Helen looked and acted very distraught, which was consistent with her circumstances. Nevertheless, she remained polite—deferential even—throughout our lengthy conversation. She needed my help, and also, it appeared, my sympathy.

Helen composed herself quickly and began, "This whole thing started on June 18th. I got a phone call from the director of Katie's [pre]school, The Discovery Zone. The director is a woman named Cecily Ogilvie-Struff. She called me and said that Katie had been behaving in a sexually inappropriate manner and had been caught touching her vagina. And when the teacher asked her to stop, Katie refused, saying her mommy does it to her at home. I guess at the time I didn't realize how bad that sounded, 'My mommy does it to me.' "

Helen paused for a moment and I seized the opportunity to interject a quick question, "Why didn't you get counseling for Katherine?"

"Oh, I did. Katie had been in therapy with a child psychologist, Dr. Claire Jansson, since April. That's what's funny. Cecily wanted me to tell Dr. Jansson about what happened in the schoolyard but I told her she should call Dr. Jansson herself. So she could hear it 'straight from the horse's mouth,' so to speak. Dr. Jansson didn't think the latest incident was that big a deal, but she reported it to [the Mendocino County Department of] Child Protective Services anyways, which she had to, by law." (Child Protective Services [CPS] is the state agency entrusted with the protection of children in California.)

"Three days later, I was sitting at home reading *Dr. Jobb's Journal*—it's a nerdy computer journal—when the doorbell rang. It was two social workers from CPS and a policeman, who identified himself as Mark Popper. I had no idea what they wanted."

"You must have had some idea," I suggested, expecting that she'd confess a mild culpability.

"No. I had no clue," she responded with evident sincerity. "I thought it might be about the school incident, but I couldn't imagine why they'd be making such a big deal about it. I asked the policeman what was going on and he said they were investigating me for sexually molesting a 'five-year-old minor, one Katherine Cross.' He really said that. Like she wasn't my daughter! The whole thing was so preposterous, I couldn't believe it was happening.

"The social workers told me they were going to interview Katie, and then they took her into the bedroom. The policeman read me my [Miranda] rights and started asking me questions. By then, it was clear to me that he wasn't on my side. So I said I wanted my lawyer present. Of course, I didn't *have* a lawyer. I never needed one before. I guess he didn't want to question me anyway, 'cause he just dropped it and we sat there in silence.

"Finally, the social workers came out from Katie's bedroom. One of them, Marcia Osborn, said that she thought Katie was sexually precocious and then the other one, Matt Bickel, said how surprised—no, he said *shocked*—how shocked he was that Katie knew the meaning of words like 'vagina' and 'penis.' I was pretty flabbergasted at that point. I told them *I* taught her those words. Marcia Osborn actually looked relieved, but the other one, Bickel, said accusingly, 'What else did you teach her? She says you touched her vagina.' Then he said he'd find out what was 'really going on' and intimated that I was going to lose my daughter.

"At that point I knew I was fighting a losing battle, but I tried to explain it to them anyway. I was treating a minor vaginal irritation with Neosporin, I said. That's all it was—Neosporin. But they didn't believe me and they took Katie away and put her in a foster home."

After finishing this emotional tale, Helen gave me a few sketchy details on how she got Katherine back and on the status of her still-pending case, and then abruptly ended the conversation with a plaintive look on her face. Previously animated, now she seemed shy and reserved.

"Could you, *please* be an expert witness for me?" she pleaded. "My little girl is my whole life. I couldn't live without her. And I didn't do anything. If you could just testify . . ."

Could I? I still wasn't sure. If I were going to testify on her behalf, I'd need to be absolutely convinced that she was innocent. I told her the truth—that I wasn't sure, but I would certainly think about it. I promised to contact her in the next few days.

Helen left me with all the relevant documents in the case thus far, including reports from the police and Child Protective Services, and the phone numbers of all the attorneys involved in the case. I spent the next several days poring over these documents, vainly trying to glean the truth from the written page. Was it true? Had Helen really molested her daughter? If not, why were the authorities erecting a monumental case on scant evidence? Mother-daughter incest is an extremely rare occurrence. Surely, Child Protective Services knew that. And a wrongful arrest and forced separation could have severe psychological consequences for both Helen and her daughter. Surely they knew that too.

One thing was clear: Helen's case was much more complicated than she had originally implied. It was not an open and shut case of wrongful arrest. The evidence was ambiguous, on both sides. A hearing had been scheduled to determine, once and for all, if the charges against Helen were true. Until then, Katherine had been placed back in Helen's home, but official custody was still under the jurisdiction of Child Protective Services.

THE POLICE REPORT

The initial police report, dated June 21, 1997, stated that Helen was being charged with "lewd and lascivious acts with a child under fourteen years of age (California Penal Code 288a)." The report indicated that Child Protective Services had initiated its investigation following the phone call from Katherine's therapist, Dr. Jansson, regarding her acting out at school. As part of the investigation, CPS contacted The Discovery Zone, where they were informed of Katherine's "preoccupation with her private parts, excessive masturbation, and exposing herself to other children." Although sexual behaviors of this sort are quite common among children and need not unduly concern parents and caretakers, the CPS investigators were also aware that, in some instances, sexual misbehaviors are a symptom of premature sexualization or sexual abuse. In Katherine's case they were not overly alarmed until they spoke with Lisa DeVries, one of Katherine's teachers, who described her efforts to stop Katherine from raising her dress and masturbating with a little boy. "Katie, why do you do these things?" she asked. To which Katherine reportedly replied, "Mommy does it to me at home."

As a consequence of these allegations, police officer Mark Popper was dispatched to Helen Cross's house, together with two CPS investigators, Marcia Osborn and Matt Bickel. After gaining entrance, Osborn and Bickel led Katherine to a separate room where Osborn briefly interviewed her (apparently Bickel remained silent throughout the interview), while Popper stayed with Helen. First, Osborn asked Katherine if she'd like to play a game and showed her a doll. Katherine agreed, and Osborn asked her if she could name the doll's private body parts. Katherine raised the doll's dress, pointed to the genital region, and said, "this is vagina." "Vagina," she explained, was a word her mommy taught her.

Then, Osborn told Katherine they were going to play another game, in which the doll would be Katherine, and Katherine would pretend to be the mommy. The police report states that "Katherine took the doll and said, 'Mommy does like this,' " while rubbing her thumb against the doll's pubic area. Then Katherine told the CPS investigator that her mother opens her legs apart and demonstrated on the doll, holding the legs wide open. She also told Osborn that "it is done on mommy's bed," that her panties are taken off, and that "mommy puts aspirin in." When Osborn asked her what color the aspirin was, Katherine replied that it was white. And when she was asked how big it was, she held her hands approximately two to three inches apart. But, when asked if she knew what aspirin was, Katherine said no.

"And does your mommy put anything else on your vagina?" asked Osborn. "Yes," said Katherine, "medicine." When queried further about the "medicine," Katherine made a motion as if squeezing something out a tube against the doll's vaginal area.

According to Katherine, the medicine was white and her mother put it on her whenever her vagina hurt. The CPS investigator pursued the topic of "hurt," looking for further evidence of traumatic abuse. When she asked Katherine, "Does anyone hurt your vagina?" Katherine replied, "yes, somebody." Osborn continued, "Who hurts you?" Katherine, perhaps tiring of this particular "game," became flustered, "I forget . . . I don't remember . . . No one does . . . When my vagina hurts . . ." The CPS worker then asked her, "When does your vagina hurt?" But Katherine again responded that she didn't remember.

Osborn reassured Katherine that everything was okay and that she wasn't going to get into trouble just by talking with her. Once Katherine seemed calm again, Osborn handed her a note pad and a crayon and asked her to draw the "aspirin" that her mother placed "in" her vagina. Katherine drew a line approximately five to six inches long. When the CPS investigator asked Katherine how wide it was, she made the "OK" sign, and, when asked how it felt, she replied that it was "soft and cold." This concluded the interview with Katherine, who was told to stay in her room.

After briefly conferring with Popper in the hallway, Osborn and Bickel rejoined Helen in the living room. Osborn sat down in a chair opposite Helen and told her that their investigation had been prompted by Katherine's inappropriate behavior at school, plus allegations that Helen was involved. Helen was flabbergasted. Her conduct toward her daughter had always been entirely appropriate and nonsexual, she insisted. Osborn replied that Katherine had intimated otherwise: that Helen had put ointment on her in an arousing manner, thereby encouraging masturbation.

Helen balked! "Neosporin? Is that what all this is about? I used Neosporin on her when she had a vaginal irritation, but I *never* touched her vagina directly. I would squeeze the tube over the irritation!"

"Well, that's not all!" Bickel exclaimed, "There's other stuff too. Her behavior's not normal and we know she has to be getting it somewhere." Helen calmly stated that she was aware of Katherine acting out sexually (she did it at home as well as at school) and emphasized that it was *she* who brought it to the attention of Katherine's teachers, rather than the reverse. Helen explained that she had first noticed an increase in Katherine's sexual playing after an incident at a friend's house during the previous Thanksgiving. Katherine and a little boy were playing in a bedroom. Helen and the boy's mother became concerned when they couldn't hear any talking and went to investigate. When they opened the door, Katherine was sitting on a pillow with her panties down, and was bleeding slightly from a scratch on the outer labia of her vagina. When Helen asked what had happened, the little boy proudly announced that he "did it." Katherine was taken to the doctor the next day. The scratch, he said, was probably caused by a fingernail.

Osborn asked Helen if she knew of any other instances of possible molestation. Helen said she didn't have any proof, but that she no longer left her daughter at their neighbor's house because she suspected that her babysitter's husband, John Lopes, might have "acted inappropriately" with Katherine.

Both Osborn and Popper made notations in their field notebooks recording the possibility of an additional suspect. But Bickel seemed not to be paying attention to Helen's testimony. "Well, are we going to do this, or not?" he asked Osborn impatiently. Without a word, Osborn arose and went to retrieve Katherine from her bedroom.

Katherine was taken away, crying, "Mommy! Mommy! I don't want to go!" Helen feebly tried to reassure her, "It's okay. . . . It's okay. . . . Mommy will see you soon."

Hours later, Helen remained curled up on the couch, clutching her knees to her chest, and quietly crying, "I've lost my child . . . Oh my god, I've lost my child!"

The next day Osborn and Popper interviewed Lopes, who worked part time as an automobile mechanic in Fort Bragg. His wife Mary sat by his side throughout the interview. After reading him his Miranda rights, they told Lopes that his name had come up in the course of an ongoing investigation. Lopes appeared irritated. "Why am I being investigated?" he asked insistently. He was assured that it was just routine. Then Popper asked him if "he had ever had touched Katherine Cross in a way that she might misinterpret."

Lopes was no fool. He must have known what was happening. This was *not* "routine questioning"—it was a molestation investigation. "No," he answered, "I never touched Katherine in any way."

"Were you ever alone with her?" Popper asked.

"No. And anyways I don't think you . . ."

By then, his wife Mary had become visibly agitated. She interrupted her husband's fumbling response and explained that John was never left alone with the children she babysat, and wasn't even around most of the time, only at lunch.

Surprisingly, Osborn and the police officer did not pursue this curious tidbit (*why wasn't he ever left alone with them?*), but instead concluded their questioning. Mary and John Lopes were officially dismissed as suspects.

After interviewing Lopes, Popper and Osborn drove back to Katherine's preschool to interview her former teacher, Lisa DeVries, who shared the following story with them: A while back, DeVries observed Katherine lifting up her dress, showing her underwear to a little boy, and then "taking the little boy's hand in her hand and guiding it to her private parts." DeVries approached the children and cautioned them that "those are special private parts and we do not do that at school." But Katherine seemed unconcerned, replying, "We do it at home, my mom puts medicine on me and it feels real good and gooshy when I pull my panties up." Then, Katherine "went skipping on her way, playing with the other kids as if nothing was wrong."

MENDOCINO

After reading the reports, I was hooked. I *had* to find some answers. My gut feeling told me that Helen was probably innocent and that the whole case was built on a simple misunderstanding, caused by a preschooler's inability to express herself clearly. But why, then, were Child Protective Services and the police so intent on believing that Helen had molested her daughter?

And what, if anything, were John and Mary Lopes trying to hide? Why *shouldn't* John Lopes be left alone with children? And why was Mary so quick to deny that he ever was?

I decided to become more actively involved in the case. But first, I needed to get more information from Helen Cross. So it was off to Mendocino, Helen's home town. After wrapping up some loose ends at UCLA, I grabbed a commuter flight to San Francisco, rented a black Lincoln towncar, and headed north on the winding and wooded Pacific Coast Highway.

Mendocino is a picturesque fishing village about three hours north of San Francisco. It sits high on a bluff overlooking the dramatic Pacific coastline. It also borders a magnificent, old-growth redwood forest that exudes a sweet piney scent which competes with the salty Pacific breezes. The town itself is quaint in the purest sense of the word. The streets are dotted with ornately decorated Victorian homes, holdovers from the previous century, when Mendocino was a thriving outpost of civilization in the forests of Northern California. Helen lived in one such home, just a short walk from the center of town.

I drove up to Helen's house and parked the rental car under a towering eucalyptus tree. Helen greeted me at the door with a hesitant smile and a worried look on her face. After making myself comfortable in her modestly furnished living room, I asked her once again to tell me her side of the story.

Helen hesitated slightly: "I have never sexually molested my daughter. I am a concerned mother. I try to be conscientious. When Katherine was having problems at school—sexually acting out—I put her in therapy. Do you think that if I was trying to hide something, that I would put her in therapy?"

But what about Katherine's allegations? What about the "medicine"?

Matter-of-factly, Helen told me that Katherine often complained of vaginal irritation, and when she did, Helen either squeezed ointment on it, or told Katherine to take a bath. Helen reassured me that she does not touch Katherine's vagina. She simply squeezes Neosporin directly from the tube onto the irritated spot. This raised another question in my mind: *why* couldn't she put medication directly on Katherine's vagina? After all, if Katherine's knee were irritated, she wouldn't avoid touching her daughter's knee, would she? So I asked her: why *not* apply the medicine directly? Helen understood the paradox, but couldn't answer. "I just wouldn't . . . I just wouldn't," she stammered. This response—stammering and all—seemed to be the right answer.

The conversation, which continued for two more hours, soon turned to Helen's life circumstances: her job, Kather-

ine's father, and so forth. Helen told me that she had just
turned forty-three. She has a Ph.D. in electrical engineering
from Stanford University, and designs microprocessor cir-
cuits for an electronics company in nearby Fort Bragg.

Helen was married once, when she was nineteen, to a
bead-wearing '60s holdover named Tony. The marriage
lasted a scant four years. Katherine, however, is not Tony's
daughter, but is instead the unplanned-but-definitely-wanted
consequence of an affair Helen had many years later with a
local businessman named Peter. Like Helen, Peter was
blonde, good-looking, and educated. He was also married. It
was a passionate if short-lived relationship that came to a
bitter end when Peter's wife caught her husband and Helen
behind his desk, *flagrante delicto.*

Naturally, Helen got pregnant. Childless, and thirty-eight
years old, Helen considered the pregnancy an act of God.
She decided to keep the child. Peter, though now getting a divorce, did not want to marry Helen or to raise a child. After
Katherine was born, Helen went back to graduate school to
finish her doctoral studies. Later, she returned to Mendocino, diploma in one hand, daughter in the other.

Helen believes that she was indicted, in part, because of
her "lifestyle." She was, after all, an unwed mother, and despite its liberal-cum-hippie legacy, Mendocino remains a
small town at heart. Helen's neighbors were not shy about
sharing their opinions regarding her work schedule, the way
she kept house, and the importance of finding a father for
Katherine. More than one neighbor was also concerned
about Helen's sexual behavior. Gossip around the neighbor-
hood intimated that Helen was "swinger," with a penchant
for *ménage à trois.* Helen, for her part, did not deny this ac-

cusation when I asked her if it was true. "I've done a lot of experimenting," she said, "but I would never do anything to harm my daughter."

We decided it was time to call it quits. Throughout our interview, and the phone conversations before that, I had been careful not to overtly encourage Helen, nor to discourage her either. I needed her to be honest with me.

Before leaving, I reminded Helen that I still needed to talk with Katherine, but agreed to do it later, on another trip to Mendocino, within the next few weeks. I'd also need to talk to her neighbors and to Katherine's teachers. But that too could wait. I encouraged Helen to collect all the documents that she thought were relevant to her case—those that seemed harmful as well as those that supported her position—and to send them to me in L.A.

After I boarded the plane back to L.A. and settled into my seat, I began to review the case in my head. Something seemed to be missing. The police report was oblique. And I still wasn't fully convinced of Helen's credibility. Both sources seemed inadequate.

SEXUAL ABUSE AND THE COURTS

The inconsistencies in the police report were especially troubling. In it, Katherine changes her story several times. At one point, it seems like mother-daughter incest. Later, it reads like treatment of a vaginal irritation. Which part should I believe? Is aspirin a white object, two to three inches long, that is rubbed against, or inserted in the vagina? Or is it a medicinal cream? Katherine says it's one, then the other, or she says she doesn't know. Was she simply confused or did she somehow realize the implications of her story? Could she read it in the disapproving faces of the social workers?

Equally troubling are the broader implications of Katherine's testimony. Like other professionals in the area of child abuse, I try always to follow the dictum, "first believe the child." When viewed historically, the adoption of this guideline by professionals throughout the Western world is a major achievement. Children have been telling tales of sexual abuse for a long time, but only recently have we begun to listen. Now there are laws that require doctors, psychologists, social workers, and other professionals to report suspicions of child abuse, or risk criminal charges. Moreover, many law-enforcement officials now receive special training for the detection and treatment of child abuse.

In general, people don't want to hear about the sexual molestation of children. It's unfathomable. It's disgusting. It's vicious and exploitative. Many parents would rather avoid the subject, and refuse to listen to their children's accusations, because it is too overwhelming. Women, especially, are loathe to entertain the possibility that the man they love—their child's father—could commit such an atrocity. And for many years, the police also disbelieved reports of child abuse, or, like other professionals, were persuaded to ignore it. Judges, too, stood unconvinced, especially when "fine, upstanding citizens" were accused—and they often were.

Fortunately, times have changed. The American public has been flooded with evidence of the pervasiveness of child abuse and molestation. It can, and does happen. And the typical abuser is not mentally deranged or otherwise exceptional. Abusers can be found throughout the entire spectrum of professional and nonprofessional ranks, including both men and women, welfare moms and notable celebrities. Sexual abusers can be parents, relatives, neighbors, teachers, police officers, and sometimes, strangers. And although most sexual abusers of children are men, women may also be involved—either as abusers themselves, willing accomplices, or through neglect or disbelief of their children.

Now that the pervasiveness of sexual abuse is recognized, steps can be taken to limit its occurrence, and to provide support, treatment, and sympathy for its victims. Many parents and public officials are now trained to recognize potential sexual abusers, and children are taught to distinguish between "good touching" and "bad touching," and to shout "No!" when bad touching occurs. (Research indicates that many potential sexual abusers will leave an assertive child alone.)

Moreover, a record number of child abusers are being apprehended and prosecuted, thanks largely to society's heightened awareness of this tragic social malady, and its increased willingness to address this issue, no matter how distasteful it may be. Arrests and convictions are both up, ensuring that more child abusers are punished than ever before.

Unfortunately, mistakes also sometimes occur. As a consequence, some abusers remain free when they belong in jail, while innocent men and women are charged, prosecuted, and imprisoned. Sexual abuse is difficult to detect and even more difficult to prove, especially when the victim is a young child. Sometimes there is physical evidence, but usually not. Some children are cooperative, others won't discuss it. The general rule of thumb is to trust the child, to assume that the child is telling the truth. And most of the time, this is sufficient.

MOTHER-DAUGHTER INCEST

As a sex researcher, I know that the probability that a mother would be sexually involved with her five-and-a-half year old daughter is a million to one. I could not find a single documented case of mother-daughter incest that did not involve either a psychotic or emotionally disturbed mother (or a mercenary one with affiliations to child pornography or prostitution). Instead, in the dozen or so documented cases of nonfinancially motivated abuse of which I am aware, the mother is usually characterized as being emotionally needy and dependent upon her children for emotional support, or as suffering from a psychological disturbance. Most of these mothers physically abuse their children as well as sexually abuse them. Typically, the sexual abuse begins when the daughter is very young (five years old or younger) and involves genital touching and masturbation, voyeuristic activities, and occasionally, insertion of objects into the daughter's vagina.

Overall, it has been estimated that only about 5% of all cases of childhood sexual abuse (not confined to incest) are perpetrated by women acting alone. Very, very few of these cases could be characterized as mother-child incest, and even fewer as mother-daughter incest. However, many cases of incest probably go unreported, as with all forms of sexual abuse. Mother-child incest may be especially problematic in this regard because the closeness of the mother-child relationship and the intimate nature of maternal activities, such as bathing and dressing the child, may make it difficult for the child or others to recognize when a boundary has been crossed and abuse has occurred.

In sum, it was *possible* that the allegations about Helen were true, but if so, this would be an incredibly rare case. Helen appeared to be psychologically well-adjusted and therefore an unlikely perpetrator of mother-daughter incest. Moreover, there were no signs that Katherine had been physically abused. Cases of incest involving mothers without overt psychological disturbances undoubtedly do exist, but for whatever reason they haven't been properly documented in the clinical literature. Thus, the "base rates" were definitely in Helen's favor.

But the evidence, especially the police reports, were decidedly *not* in Helen's favor. Was she telling the truth and were the police, who seemed to feel the evidence of abuse to be incontrovertible, making a huge mistake? Unfortunately, at that time, I couldn't tell who was right and who was wrong. There simply wasn't enough evidence. I was hoping that the gynecological report would provide some much needed answers.

GYNECOLOGICAL EVIDENCE

Several days later, while grading papers in my office at UCLA, I received a fax from Dr. Nancy Dworkin, the gynecologist who examined Katherine. Unfortunately, rather than lending clarity to the confusion, her report only muddied the waters further. Many of Dr. Dworkin's findings were ambiguous and could be interpreted in multiple ways, although she seemed oblivious to the alternatives. For example, she discovered a small area of irritation on Katherine's labia, which she interpreted as "*prima facia* evidence of molestation.*" The possibility that the irritation might have been caused by masturbation or perhaps by sexual play with another youngster was not broached in the official report. In this and other instances, Dr. Dworkin seemed to be jumping to extreme conclusions, as though she were presupposing molestation and looking for confirmatory evidence. She concluded in no uncertain terms that molestation had occurred, despite a complete lack of evidence of vaginal or anal penetration (Katherine's hymen was intact). At the very least, it appeared that Dr. Dworkin was overstating the facts.

In psychology, we have a saying: "Expectancy is a self-fulfilling prophecy." When you expect something, you tend to find evidence to support it. For example, if you believe lawyers are greedy you will find evidence to support this hypothesis. Expectations are thus a form of bias, or prejudice, and therefore the enemy of truth and science.

To circumvent such biases, psychologists try to minimize expectations by "blinding" subjects to our hypotheses. For instance, in Katherine's case, we would not tell the gynecologist that Katherine was a suspected victim of molestation, for fear of creating expectations on her part. Instead, we would just ask for a complete and thorough physical and gynecological exam. In this manner, the physician's conclusions would not be influenced by prior beliefs or expectations. And as a consequence, different interpretations could be entertained. This objectivity is the core of the scientific method.

Police and social workers play by a different set of rules, however. Objectivity is secondary to results. In Helen's case, they wanted evidence of sexual abuse, and they wanted Dr. Dworkin to find it. "Was there any evidence to suggest that Katherine was victim of sexual molestation?" they had asked Dr. Dworkin. Her answer, not surprisingly, was yes, there was. Dr. Dworkin reported finding a "generalized erythema in the inner labial area," and "mild hyperpigmentation and thickening over the external labia majora." Simply stated, certain parts of the labia around the vagina were red, and perhaps irritated. This condition, she concluded, was "consistent with molestation."

The remainder of the report, however, was inconsistent with abuse. First, there was no evidence of penetration in either the recent or distant past. The hymenal ring diameter was six millimeters, which is too small to admit a moistened Q-Tip. The hymen was thick and normal texture for Katherine's age. There were no bruises, lacerations, or contusions on any part of her body. Katherine was a healthy, well-nourished young girl.

I thought about this report for several days before deciding to do a simple experiment. I would see if I could replicate Dr. Dworkin's results by having a gynecologist I know at UCLA examine the medical report. Replication is the heart of observational science, after all. One person observes a phenomenon, others confirm (or disconfirm) it through repeated examinations.

In this spirit I contacted a colleague of mine in the medical school, Dr. James Mbidde, who is a board-certified gynecologist. I asked him to help me with a case, but told him nothing about Katherine's situation. I faxed him only the medical findings. The next day he called me with his interpretations. According to Dr. Mbidde, the "generalized erythema in the inner labial area could indicate a yeast infection; contact dermatitis; or an allergy to dies, soaps, or medication," whereas the "mild hyperpigmentation and thickening over the external labia majora" observed by Dr. Dworkin was probably caused by "chronic scratching or frequent masturbation." Unlike Dr. Dworkin, who was explicitly searching for evidence of molestation, Dr. Mbidde found none.

For the first time, I began to believe Helen at a rational level, bringing my mind in alignment with my instincts. I still wasn't sure, but the most damaging evidence, the only *physical* evidence—Dr. Dworkin's gynecological report—had been rebutted. But even as one conflict abated, another erupted.

Dr. Mbidde is an expert, but Dr. Dworkin is certainly competent as well. So why didn't she suggest masturbation as a possible cause of the irritation she observed around Katherine's labia, either instead of, or in conjunction with, molestation? In her report, she acknowledges that "teachers were concerned about Katherine's markedly increased masturbation," so she was not unaware of this potential cause. What about an allergic reaction to medication, such as Neosporin? Once again, Dr. Dworkin acknowledges that Katherine "had stated that her mother had put cream on her vagina." Why weren't these alternative explanations explored?

Perhaps Dr. Dworkin had been lead astray by false expectations. She found evidence of abuse because she expected to find evidence of abuse. In any event, the evidence of molestation wasn't strong, yet the police and Child Protective Services persisted. Why? Was something more going on? Perhaps Helen knew. Was she concealing something? Or were hidden agendas being played out at her expense?

I needed more information about Helen, Katherine, and the incidents that led to the arrest. I also needed more information on the bit players in this little drama. To get these facts, I needed to visit Mendocino again.

A SMALL-TOWN GIRL
FROM SOUTH DAKOTA

After checking in at the MacCallum House, a pricey bed and breakfast in the center of town, I walked over to Ruby's, a small cafe run by an old friend of Helen's. Ruby's featured an old, depression-era counter straight out of Edward Hopper's famous painting, *Nighthawks*. The stainless steel counter coolly reflected the bright lights that lit up the otherwise somber cafe.

I arrived just minutes before Helen. We grabbed a booth and ordered coffee and a slice of homemade rhubarb pie. My plan was to get a quick history, then press her for information on the local authorities, including the Mendocino police and Child Protective Services.

It didn't work out that way. Helen is a great talker. And I am a good listener. During the course of the evening, I believe she told me the better part of her life story. Here's how it began:

"I was born in Custer, South Dakota. My parents were poor. I was the seventh child of ten children. My parents were just regular people. Not well-educated or interested in culture. Never went beyond the eighth grade. But they were hard-working people, who trusted others.

"My father was in the construction business. He was a hod carrier. In case you don't know what a hod carrier is— they mix up cement, and carry it to the bricklayer. It is hard manual labor. He also worked on a ranch.

"My mother worked sometimes. Sometimes not. But when each of my parents worked, it was long hours. During the summer, my father put in ten hours a day. In the heat and humidity. In the winter, there wasn't much opportunity for a hod carrier. So we'd have money in the summer, and nothing in winter.

"My father was a drinker. When he was broke, during the winter, his drinking would increase. But he would also drink during the summer. After work, the guys would go out to a saloon. My father would drink a lot of beer. I don't remember him drinking anything else.

"My mother didn't drink. No, that's not true—I've seen her drink a little beer. Not usually a whole one. And only once in a while. It wasn't something she liked. She preferred soft drinks. Like me. I don't usually drink. Someone will offer me a beer, every now and then, and I'll drink some. I don't like drinking a whole can. If I do drink, it's usually at a party. It helps me relax. But I still have a good time when I don't drink. And people can't tell the difference. I go into party mode whether I'm drinking or not.

"But, back to my family. As I've said, they were poor. Things were always at a crisis. Even when money was coming in, we still had accumulated debts. I remember bill collectors coming. Things being repossessed.

"My mother had middle-class values. The belief that hard work paid off. Abide by the law. Be kind to your neighbor. All of that. She was very dedicated to her children. Her first child died shortly after birth. Ten more lived. She put all of her energy into us. That was my model. But I think I fought against it for a long time. I didn't like the image of wife and mother that I saw growing up.

"My father felt children were mother's job. He was drinking, and sleeping with other women, when each of us were born. I forgive him now. After seeing years of human foibles, I take another perspective. It was his way of relieving the stress of having another mouth to feed. Of course, my mother had stresses. But she didn't get that kind of release.

"All of us children were two years apart in age. Our mother nursed us for a long time—one year. The lactation may have delayed ovulation. That was probably their only birth control. My mother had her first child when she was seventeen. The last at thirty-eight. I was born when my mother was thirty-four. I am closest to my only sister, Nancy, who is two years older, and my brother, Ken, who is two years younger. The three of us grew up together. We had a strong dedication to each other. The rest of my siblings were kind of invisible to me.

"Nancy is very domestic. She would stay inside and help my mother since she was older. Nancy would cook and help clean up. But not me. I didn't want to cook, or do things of that sort. I fought the traditional female role. But Nancy, she is more like my mother. She has five grown children. Really nice kids. Also, she has three grandchildren. In fact, she became a grandmother before I became a mother. You can see how long I fought the traditional female role.

"Except for Nancy and Ken, I don't have much in common with the rest of my siblings. Some were married when I was still a little girl. I also don't like their values. They have a lot of racist and sexist attitudes. It's nauseating to me—and to Nancy and Ken too.

"My mother would say racist things about Native Americans. But basically, she had respect for everybody. All of us always knew that we were loved by our mother. She loved us all equally. Now, I joke with her about it. Saying, 'You had to do it that way. But if you loved one best, it would be me.' Of course this wasn't true. She never singled us out. The most handsome son got the same praise as the least handsome.

"My father was democratic in his child rearing too. *Every* child was ignored. He showed no warmth. The only bond was complaining. Complain about the mayor, and if my father agreed, he would show you attention. Join in. But not affection. One of the only times that I remember my father showing affection was when Ken was being bitten by some roosters. Ken was very small, and we lived way out in the country. My father ran out of the house and grabbed the roosters by the neck and spun them around. When he was done, there were four dead roosters laying in the yard. When I think of my father's love, that's what pops into my head. He was showing his love, by killing chickens!

"As an adult, I looked at my father differently. I realized how hard it is to earn a living in the Black Hills of South Dakota. How hard it is to get ahead. How easy it is for a man to run away from his family. But my father never seemed to think of that. And I had to respect him for it. Not love him, but respect him.

"When I left home at seventeen to go to the University of South Dakota, I hated my father. Some time later, I stopped thinking about him. And as I grew older, and started feeling a love for all mankind, I extended that love to my father, as one more person in the world. A basic love for the human

condition. Life is hard, and my father is another human being who has struggled with the questions: What is the meaning of life? Why am I a stranger and afraid in a world I never
made? And so on. That kind of thing.

"But, truth be told, I hated my father for another reason.
When I was twelve years old, he told me to come up to the
attic. He was very drunk. He made me sit on his lap. Talking
to me, he started rubbing my breasts. I was very frightened.
It didn't last very long and it never happened again. But it
changed things. I became very distant to him. And he ignored me even more. A similar incident happened with my
sister Nancy.

"But I forgave my father. One night, many years later, I
was living with a boyfriend in San Francisco. I woke up at
2 a.m. crying. It was like a religious experience, but I don't
consider it religious. Maybe it was a peak experience, very
strange and unusual. Anyway, I was crying, but got out of
bed. I felt driven. I walked into the back bedroom, turned on
the light, and started writing. Words flowed from my pen.
As if not from me, and yet, very deeply from me—from my
core. It was a long, poorly written, poorly structured, free-
form poem to my father. I wasn't trying to write it beauti-
fully. Or do anything with it. You'll think this is silly, but it
said: 'A long time ago, all of this had happened, and it was
ugly, sinful. It was terrible. But it was over a long time before.' I told my father (in this poem) to live out his life without ever thinking about what happened in the attic. I wanted
it to end for him. And if he ever felt regret, guilt, or shame
about what happened to Nancy and I, plus all of the suffering we went through as children—I wanted him to forget it,
and put it behind him. And spend whatever years he had left

enjoying himself. Doing whatever he wanted to do. Be a husband to my mother. And never think about it again. I forgave him. I wanted my father to live out the rest of his life purged of this experience. And you know, strangely enough, the last twelve years of his life (he died last year) were that way. My mother's image of my father, to this day, is of a man who was very thoughtful. Always telling her how wonderful and beautiful she was. Because, that's what my father did, for the last twelve years of his life. And to me, it's okay if she doesn't remember anything else. To her, that was the 'true' man—those last twelve years. And she loved that man. So, it's okay, at least by me, that I will never love him. But I'm glad that they had those last twelve years.

"After writing that poem my nightmares stopped. For much of my life, I've had bad dreams. Horrible, recurring nightmares. About a man. A sinister, scary force. Or my father. In a demeaning, horrible sexual situation. Or just impending doom. Horror that I couldn't escape. Sometimes, the dreams were repeated in the same night. But, it almost seems strange to talk about them now. It was so long ago. And they finally stopped when I forgave my father—that free-floating horror just went away.

"So, that night marked the end of a long process of coming to terms with what had happened to me. Not only the incestuous part, but the drinking, the ugliness, the deprivation of my childhood. It marked a time of transition. I put it all behind me. I feel healthier accepting my father, and removing the image of him as a monster. I think that in owning him again, I've taken back part of myself.

"It's interesting, since this recent horror with my daughter I've realized, once again, how important it is to get over the effects of molestation, or rape, or incest. To get to the point where you can forgive. And for me, it wasn't something I planned. I didn't know that I was going to forgive. It just happened. And to some extent, I just sat and looked at the experience."

It was nearly two in the morning when Helen finished, and I, for one, was starved. Ruby was asleep on a couch, so we cooked some eggs and home fries and served ourselves. After eating, we paid the bill, agreed to meet again the next day, and left, in silence.

As Helen drove off, I walked back to the bed and breakfast. It was after hours, so I fished out my key and let myself in. I went upstairs and sat silently in my room trying to sort things out. Hours passed, and soon it was morning. I napped until noon, then called Helen, explaining that perhaps it would be better if we waited until later in the evening—when we could talk over drinks—rather than meeting for lunch. She acquiesced without complaint.

HELEN'S STORY

Incest and other forms of sexual molestation occur with frightening regularity. Statistical studies indicate that indi-

viduals who were victims as children are more likely to
be victimizers as adults. According to one prominent theory, victims of childhood sexual abuse are "socialized" into
the adult role of abuser because their experiences have "nor-
malized" adult-child sex. Thus, they no longer believe that
adult-child sex is wrong because doing so would pathologize
their childhood experiences. Another theory posits that victims suffer from a compulsion to repeat the traumatic experience as a way to overcome or relieve it.

Presuming, for the moment, that Helen is telling the truth
about the incest with her father, the most striking aspect of
her story was her willingness to tell it. Most people accused
of serious crimes make a verbal retreat. They become suspicious and paranoid (perhaps rightfully so) and either with-
hold information, or sanitize it in such a way as to create a
favorable impression. Helen, evidently, is not operating on
this principle. She is a very smart woman, and well aware of
the connection between childhood victimization and adult
perpetration of sexual abuse. Yet, in the service of telling the
"truth," she did not eliminate this potentially incriminating
detail.

Helen was clearly a survivor, and indeed, with regard to
educational and professional achievement, an extraordinarily successful woman. She appears to have both guts and determination. She also is an extremely passionate person—
this was clear from our first conversation. Helen is an emotional seeker who is continually looking for life's answers in
order to overcome her own insecurity, dissatisfaction, and
distrust. These personal characteristics are not surprising
given her family's interpersonal dynamics. On the other
hand, Helen seemed relatively straightforward, unwilling to

mask either the dysfunction of her family or the blemishes it had left on her. This, in my business, is a good sign.

That evening I met Helen at a local pub—a place called the Mine Shaft—that featured microbrewed ales from the Mendocino Brewing Company. I had hoped a beer would help Helen relax, so she could speak openly about her relationship with Katherine and the alleged sexual abuse. As it turned out, she didn't need any prompting, alcoholic or otherwise. She was quite willing, even relieved, to discuss her situation and her recent difficulties with her daughter.

After a half hour of small talk, the conversation quite naturally came around to Katherine and her "acting out at school." I asked Helen to elaborate.

"Well, it began about a year and a half ago, around Thanksgiving. Thanksgiving sticks out in my mind because we were over at a friend's—Mary Lopes's—house for turkey dinner. Katie and Ben, who is the same age, had been playing. They were quiet, and when a mother becomes aware that her child is quiet, she goes and checks. A few days before, they had dumped toys into the aquarium, and that's what we were afraid of. But instead, Katie and Ben were on the bed. He had his clothes on, but Katherine's pants were down. And as I walked towards her, I saw that there was blood on the pillow. I think they were four years old at the time. Katie was crying, and she was blaming Ben for it. I took her into the bathroom to stop the blood, because I thought that it was frightening her. The next day, when I took her to the doctor, she had a scratch on her labia.

"Mary felt guilty, like it was her fault, so she became

overly cautious. On the following day, when she was babysitting, Katie had trouble urinating, so Mary called me at work. She thought that Katie might have an infection. I thought that was very unlikely, but I took her to the doctor again. The doctor said Katie had a little scratch near her urethra (probably from the other day when she was playing with Ben), which made it sting when she tried to pee. So she was trying to avoid peeing.

"These two episodes were the first times that Katie had been examined by the doctor in that area. And the blood from the previous day was really frightening to her. When Katie eventually went to counseling, she acted out that scene with puppets and said that the girl puppet was very scared.

"Shortly after that, one of the teachers came to me, and said that Katie had been behaving sexually at school. I told her what had happened at Thanksgiving and then asked her if anything had happened right after that, or if it had been going on for a while. She said no, that it seemed to start around Thanksgiving. I thought that the trauma associated with the incident with Ben had prompted her to start acting out.

"I called the Mendocino Counseling Center and told them what was going on. I went in to see someone I had seen before, a woman named Dr. Levy. I talked it over with her and she said that her experience was not with children, and that she would discuss it with someone there, and get back with me.

"When they got back to me they said that this was something that could be handled without counseling since she had never shown any other signs of insecurities, like she had never sucked her thumb, never carried a blanket, nothing. It wasn't anything I needed to worry about, I just needed to tell her strongly that this was not appropriate behavior at school. But instead, it was something to do in private. That's what I did, and as far as I knew, that behavior died down.

"Incidentally, all of this happened when Katie was on the little kids' side of preschool. When she switched to the big kids' side, around April of the following year, I told them what had happened previously. I also asked them to tell me if the behavior started up again. I told that to the lead teacher, thinking that she would disseminate the information among the other teachers. However, I didn't go to each one individually.

"In fact, Katie wasn't assigned to the lead teacher, but was assigned to another teacher. So, I don't know when her sexual behavior started up again.

"She was on the big kids' side from April to June. There was a break during the summer, and then in September, she started back to school. I wasn't aware of anything until shortly before I contacted the Mendocino Counseling Center again, which would be in February, when Katie started going for counseling. I started counseling this time because one of the other parents told me that she had seen Katie and another kid try to pull her daughter's pants down at school.

"Since this acting out seemed to have an aggressive component, I decided Katie needed counseling. I was referred to a children's treatment center in Fort Bragg. And it was there that we met Dr. Jansson. Before I did this, I asked one of the teachers—not Katie's main teacher but another one—if she had been acting out, and she said, 'Yeah, a lot. I thought you knew about it.' I told her I didn't, that no one had told me anything. Anyways, right away, I called the center and made

arrangements to get Katie into counseling, and then in late
March or early April, she started going there. Nothing much
had come out of her counseling, as far as sexually acting out
was concerned, until, of course, this police incident happened.

"All this began when Katie was either touching her
vagina or just showing herself, I don't know which, and a
teacher said to her, 'Katherine, that's private,' and her response was, 'It's okay, mommy and I do this at home all the
time,' and she skipped away. And that's what precipitated
this whole thing. I don't know what the teacher immediately
did. I think she and some of the other teachers talked about
it, particularly with Cecily, who is the head of the school.
They all knew me for a long time and they knew that I had
sought counseling for Katie about her behavior. They think
of me as a very dedicated mother. In fact, I'm the only working mother they know who carries a beeper and cell phone
with me so that I can be reached immediately if my daughter
needs help.

"The next day they had a meeting with me and told me
about this and I said at the time, 'I think I'd like you to tell
this directly to Dr. Jansson, Katie's counselor, rather than it
going through me—given the possibility of distortions.' And
I said that there may be some things you are reluctant to say
to me, but you can say to Dr. Jansson.

"They said, 'Not really, we've told you everything, and
we'll tell her exactly the same thing.' They were convinced
that I hadn't done anything inappropriate with Katie, but
they wanted me to know what was going on.

"Then when Dr. Jansson met with them, she told them

that by law, it had to be reported. And they said, 'Well, we hoped that by telling you, that would be enough.' She said no, it had to be reported. So it was. Dr. Jansson reported it, and told the police that the teacher's report would follow. The police then contacted the teachers, since Dr. Jansson's report was second-hand information.

"A friend of mine works at the DA's office, and he began keeping a lookout for my case. However, when they took my daughter away, it hadn't reached his office. As it turns out, they can hold a child for seventy-two hours, and in my case it seems like they were not in any hurry. The weekend came, and they had only arranged for the doctor's examination on Friday—so they couldn't go through with the hearing, and it got postponed 'til Monday. Katie was away from me for more than seventy-two hours. In fact, it was the sixth day that she was finally returned to me. It was the worst six days of my life.

"When Dr. Jansson talked to me, which was a day or so before they came and took her, she said, 'You will have to be questioned,' and I said, 'Well, okay, but are they going to be talking to you first?' My understanding from talking to her was that they would come to her, and she would discuss the matter with them. Since Katie was already in counseling, they would leave it to her recommendation. But they didn't contact her, in fact no one *ever* contacted her. Dr. Jansson finally had to call them before the first court hearing. I don't know what credence they gave her, but they did agree to put a letter from her in my file. It's in there now.

"Katie was given her own county-appointed attorney. Her name is Julia Escobar. Julia interviewed Katie and then

reviewed Dr. Jansson's letter. Julia was persuaded by this letter—as was the first judge—so that Katie was returned to
me, at least temporarily, pending further investigation. If
that letter had not been allowed into court, the judge could
have kept Katherine in a shelter or a foster home until this
case is resolved, which could take months. So, at the minimum, without Dr. Jansson, I would have been missing Katie
for who knows how long. Thank goodness I had Dr. Jansson. Plus, Julia seemed open to the idea that I haven't done
anything wrong.

"Julia was also willing to take the tube of Neosporin into
the room when she interviewed Katie. When she asked her
about the 'aspirin,' Julia had the tubes in front of her and
Katie picked up the Neosporin, and said, 'This is what mom
uses on me.' Now, when Child Protective Services interviewed Katie, they used a different tactic. They didn't know
what Katie meant by the word 'aspirin,' so they asked her
'What is aspirin?' and told her to draw a picture of it. Katie
draws a tube. They think she is drawing a dildo, and presume that I'm sticking something like this into my child.
And, of course, their alarms go off. Never mind the fact that
meanwhile I'm out in the living room talking with the policeman, and I'm saying that the only time I've ever touched
my child there is to put medicine on her. 'What medicine?'
'Neosporin,' I said, and I went and got the tube. I had it out
there, but they weren't interested in it."

After a brief respite to examine local tastes in jukebox mu-
sic, we returned to our secluded booth in the back corner of
the pub. I shifted the conversation to John and Mary Lopes.

I had a nagging feeling about them. I couldn't help wondering, my mind floating back to the police reports: who were these people and what part (if any) did they play in this little drama?

Helen continued, "Interestingly enough, let me tell you the most recent allegation that has surfaced. This woman, Mary Lopes, used to live across from me, and now lives around the corner. She and her husband John have engaged in some pretty bizarre sexual activities. She told me sometime after I'd met John—whom I never trusted—that he had molested their children. This was shortly before they split up—but they got back together after he got out of prison. He had pleaded guilty to a lesser count of child harassment, not incest.

"Of course, I also mentioned that Mary's daughter was molested by her husband John. But that's a matter of court records. In fact, the police officer who was in charge of my investigation was in charge of John Lopes's as well. I didn't think that I was saying anything new.

"After John was in prison, I trusted Mary. Yet, it always seemed that strange things were going on with the kids. One time, when I went over there, Mary was standing in the kids' room, and my child and her two children were on the bed humping each other. I mean it looked like they were doing it, except they had their clothes on. And I said, 'Mary, do you see this?' And she said, 'Yeah, they are just showing they love each other.' Well, I took Katie home at that point because I didn't feel comfortable with that. And later on I talked to a few friends, and told them what had happened. It was bothering me. I felt that it's entirely inappropriate for the parent to stand there and watch—as did my friends. So,

I went back over to Mary's house, trembling, and said to her, 'If my daughter engages in this kind of behavior, and you know about it—you do whatever you want to with your children—but with Katie, without scolding her, you need to redirect her activity.' It's easy to redirect her. All you have to do is show her a book, or tell her about a game, and she switches very easily. And Mary said, 'Oh, okay.' But, you know what, I decided never to let Katie go over there again.

"I reported this to the police. Presumably they were investigating it, but I don't know if in order to get more out of Mary, they worded it more strongly than I had said it, or what. My own personal feeling about this is that Mary's a battered wife, and her children have been molested. I *now* also have this nagging hunch that maybe John got her in on it too, and she's afraid that her complicity will come out. And so, she was defensive.

"Well, a week and a half after I learned about all of this stuff, I called Mary back, and asked her what she had been saying about me to the police. 'Only the truth,' she said. I said, 'What truth is that?' So, she told me about what she heard about the school, but she didn't say anything else.

"See, my lawyer had recently told me that Mary had also told the police that I had a *ménage à trois* with two men, and that Katie had watched. It's true about the *ménage à trois*—that I had it I mean—but Katie wasn't there. I'd never let her watch me having sex. The particular experience Mary was referring to had happened about two and a half years ago. These two guys came over, one of whom I had previously dated. Mary saw them (they were very attractive guys), and came over, ostensibly to return something of Katie's. As it turned out, Mary told me later that she had picked up a 'vibe,' that these guys were interested in a 'thing.' Mary was hoping she would get invited to join in. Personally, I did not pick up any 'vibe'—and if I did feel something—I certainly would not invite Mary.

"I think what probably happened was that Mary told the police about these two guys. But the police responded that it isn't important, isn't relevant. So to make it more important, Mary said that it happened in front of Katie. Katie, as far as I know, has never seen any kind of sexual behavior between adults. And presumably, her psychological evaluation will substantiate that.

"But it really pissed me off that Mary was saying all of this stuff about me. And if anything, it was true about *her*. For example, Mary told me that John had no reservations about their children seeing everything—and I mean everything, given the kinds of things they got into. Like, John would go to places where they have something called 'glory holes.' Places where men have sex through a hole in the wall—but they can't see the guy on the other side. Mary also told me she had sex with John and his brother. And afterwards, John and his brother had sex with each other.

"Well, anyway, where my life is concerned, I try to do right, and to be open and honest about it. Which is the way I have raised Katie—to be very honest and open. But now, I think these values have caused problems for me. Since she feels free to speak her mind, to say things like 'Mommy says it's okay' or 'Mommy and I do this.' But in order to know *exactly* what she is talking about, you have to know a lot about her.

"I've made Katie my life. To me, when you have a child, you make a commitment to take care of them, to love them, and to protect them. If you are not going to do that, you might as well have an abortion. Even my schooling and profession took second place to Katie. A lot of people think that I give up too much of my career for Katie. And now they want to take her away from me?

"Luckily, Katie was returned to me after the first hearing. Although she wasn't a ward of the court, she was something court-related. They worded it that she was taken from me, but placed back. Or some such thing. That is, she has been taken away legally, but I guess I have temporary custody.

"I don't know if this will eventually go to trial. My lawyer, Sue Menken, tells me not to worry. Everything will be dropped. But I don't know. And I'm not sure if she's the best lawyer for me. She's basically a family law person—divorce, child custody, that sort of thing. Sue tells me if I admit to 'poor judgment,' they'd give me Katherine back—if only because they don't have enough foster homes. But I won't do that. That's just crazy. I'd rather fight the whole thing. But I don't know how to 'prove' that I didn't do it. They could drop the charges, but still consider me guilty. The stigma would still be there—unless I could prove otherwise.

"You know, ultimately, Katie will come to an age where *she* will be able to vindicate me. Yet, who knows whether people will even believe her. I feel like I devote so much time and energy to raising my daughter as best as I can, and now I have to deal with this nightmare."

Helen's last comments trailed off, like a whisper, and we were suddenly acutely aware of the silence. The Mine Shaft was empty and I was out of energy, though I think Helen could have continued. We agreed to meet once more, around noon the next day. I walked her to her car as we discussed where we should meet. I was hoping for some place with a little more natural beauty, and a lot less smoke. She suggested the restaurant at the Heritage House, which sounded good to me.

As Helen drove away I began to replay portions of the conversation in my mind. And the more I thought, the more energized I became. I drove back to the MacCallum House, parked the car in front, and then went for a walk in the cool night air.

In some ways, what Helen had told me was unremarkable. That she loved her daughter and had a very special relationship with her was exceedingly clear. But her sexual history troubled me. Whether it was relevant or not to Katherine's acting out, it would nevertheless be a factor. Mary Lopes, for one, had guaranteed that. She appeared to be trying to impugn Helen's character through sexual innuendo. Whether the police were doing the same was uncertain. Courts, nowadays, generally exclude testimony about sexual histories, unless they are relevant to the charges at hand. But were they? Mary Lopes had insinuated that they were by implying that Katherine had a participatory position, if only as a voyeur, in Helen's sex life.

I needed to find out more about Helen's sexual history—particularly any experiences that might be used against her in court. This would serve three purposes. First, I could form my own opinion about whether Katherine had observed Helen's *ménage à trois*. Second, I could assess whether Helen's sexual history, per se, had any relevance to the accusations against her. Finally, the way she reacted to my questions could serve as a litmus test of her candor. Sex is a highly charged, private, and potentially shameful arena. What someone is willing to disclose, and how they disclose it, says a lot about that person. Often, the sexual details matter less than the veracity, integrity, and sincerity of the presentation. Helen seemed like a very open person, but I wanted to know more.

A SEXUAL HISTORY

Helen arrived at the MacCallum House—our predesignated meeting place—at a little past noon. We got into the Lincoln and drove five miles south along the winding Pacific Coast Highway to the Heritage House, a stately old inn that is a favorite with Hollywood producers (it was even featured in the Alan Alda movie, *Same Time Next Year*). Helen led me into the restaurant and we seated ourselves in an isolated booth with a commanding view of the cliffs and the Pacific Ocean below. A waiter brought us iced tea and we settled in for another long session.

Before we began, I felt I should lay out the ground rules, such as they were. I explained to Helen that although sexual histories are usually irrelevant, Mary Lopes's testimony may have changed that. Consequently, it was important that I know about every experience that could be used against her. I also reassured her that, after thirty years as a sex researcher, there was virtually nothing she could tell me that would shock, or even surprise me. I wanted her to tell me everything, no matter how inconsequential it might seem. I would rather she inundate me with sexual irrelevancies, sexual hang-ups, and sexual mistakes, than to discover in court something of significance that she had withheld. I also made it clear to her that I would not serve as her expert witness unless I was convinced that she was telling the truth about everything, including her past sexual experiences.

Helen sat calmly through my little diatribe, with a bemused look on her face that told me that it had been wholly unnecessary.

"I had my first sexual experience when I was seventeen," she began. "I was going with a man from Spearfish who was twenty-four. When we started seeing each other, I was pretty naive. I had never even kissed or necked in a car before, and I remember being astonished at my own reaction. Kind of wondering what were the feelings I was feeling, and yet at the same time, knowing what they were. I wanted to have sex, but I was afraid of it. Afraid of the pain; afraid of what it meant to no longer be a virgin; and afraid of what he would think about me. The kind of things that go on in a girl's mind.

"Looking back, I feel very sorry for him, because I put him through some strange situations. The poor guy walked around horny all the time, because I would only go so far. Finally, one night, we were necking in the back seat of his car on a deserted road near Cheyenne Crossing. I had my dress and panties on, but I heard a strange sound, and I couldn't figure out what it was. I eventually realized that it was his zipper—and it became apparent that he was no longer touching me with his fingers. Then he pulled my panties aside and inserted himself.

"Well, in a fragment of a second, I went from being really sexually turned on to being stone-cold sober. And yet, I also thought, if it's going to happen, I might as well as relax and enjoy it. But I didn't do too well at that. Then I felt moisture all over my legs, and in my extreme inexperience, I thought that he had ejaculated—and that now, I must be pregnant! However, he hadn't come. It was just the breaking of my hymen, and the rush of blood that I felt all over me.

"Afterwards, I went home and threw away my bloody panties. Somehow, the dress didn't get bloody. He, on the other hand, tried to clean up the blood from the back of the seat of his car. He wasn't very successful, and actually ended up selling the car and getting a different one. It's funny now, but it wasn't funny at the time. We continued to see each other for several months. I would swear to myself that I would never do it again, yet I'd find myself there, in the back seat, or at a local lake, right out in the open! He always used the *coitus interruptus* technique—you know, withdrawal. And apparently he was good at it, because I didn't get pregnant.

"After I stopped seeing him, it was six months before I got involved with somebody else. Actually, by the time I got married at nineteen, I had had sex with four men prior to my husband. But it was all very straight, nothing kinky, until I moved to Dallas. One night, a man I had dated once or twice called me up and asked me if I would go to a sex party with him. I said I didn't know, that it sounded kind of scary, and I didn't want to get a disease or anything. Well, he talked about a mile a minute, and said, 'If you go, you don't have to take part if you don't want to. No one is going to make you do anything you don't want to do. It's just going to be some very pleasant couples that I've known for a long time. But I'm not allowed to come without a date, and I want to go, so would you go with me? All you have to do is take off your clothes when we're there, so that everybody else doesn't feel uncomfortable.' Well, I thought about it, or maybe I didn't think about it. Anyway, I went with him.

"It was an interesting experience. They *were* nice people, and everybody seemed to be intrigued with me, because I was the new kid on the block. I felt kind of overwhelmed. Eventually, I let all kinds of people touch me, but it was as if all my wires were down—nothing got through. I didn't feel anything. And in fact, all these sexual gyrations of people in this big room made me feel like laughing. It just looks funny when you are not involved. Everybody was trying so damned hard to have a wild time that it was just funny.

"Anyway, it was while I was in Dallas that I met Oliver. Oliver was a very important man in my life. I met him when I was twenty-six and he was a very prominent physician. Oliver liked me to have sexual experiences with other people, and he wanted me to tell him about them. He analyzed it this way: by encouraging me to do things with other people, it was his way of sending me off, and then, when I still wanted to be with him, it was supposedly my validation that I still loved him. 'If you love it, set it free,' that sort of thing.

"I remember once we were talking to this high-fashion model who lived with this eccentric artist. So, Oliver got to talking to her, and found out that she enjoyed being with other women. Oliver then asked me if she could join us in bed. I agreed, but I was surprised that he went for the idea right away, and asked her on the spot. So, like an hour later, the three of us were in bed together.

"I did this because I knew Oliver wanted to. But I found it to be real strange. She felt strange and she tasted strange. It wasn't like sex at all. It wasn't sickening or horrible, and it didn't make me feel guilty or uncomfortable. It was just strange. And it didn't make me feel sexy, except that I got kind of a contact high off of knowing that Oliver was really turned on—and that I was willing to do this for him. But other than that, it was just really strange, and not something that I cared to repeat.

"I'm trying to remember if we ever did it again. Oliver liked the idea—but I don't think that it happened with another woman. However, with a second man is another story. The first time we got involved with another man was when we lived in Mexico. Oliver had been away for two weeks, and of course, he encouraged me to be with other men. So I met this very prominent diplomat at a government party. This diplomat—wearing medals and all—saw me, and made a point of talking to me later. He was really a fascinating man and it seemed really important to him to meet me. So, I was very flattered. We saw each other a few times while Oliver was gone and became lovers. When Oliver came back, I told him about it, which turned Oliver on completely, since this guy was quite famous. So Oliver asked me to have the guy over for drinks, which I did. Oliver also wanted me to wear a snug, low cut dress, without panties. Which I also did.

"I found myself doing a very subtle job of teasing the diplomat, making him quite uncomfortable. It was kind of fun. And since I didn't have panties on, I would occasionally flash him, which eventually let him in on the idea that it was okay with Oliver. Later that night, the three of us ended up in bed together.

"But, when the three of us were together, I had trouble getting turned on. I seem to have a problem with being with two men, and concentrating on either one of them. On the other hand, I have many fantasies about doing that sort of thing, and it's always a turn-on. But in reality, it's hard for me to concentrate, and fully enjoy the experience. I was right in the middle of everything, literally, but I couldn't get into it the way I thought I should. Still, it was rather cool.

"I told you before that there weren't any other women that I was sexually involved in, but I just remembered someone else. In Houston, when I lived there, I wanted to see how I would react with a woman alone, without a man instigating it, or carrying it on. So, I made contact with a bisexual woman—this was back before it became the 'in' thing. Well, I wanted to explore, to see if I would function differently if I were alone with a woman.

"Anyway, I decided to try it with a woman. We didn't have sex per se, only kissed and petted. And I found that my reaction to her was the same thing. It was as if I were in a film with someone I didn't know and didn't particularly like. I could go through with it and it certainly didn't make me want to vomit, but it didn't feel sexual to me either.

"When I'm with a woman in that kind of circumstance, it doesn't feel right. I'm amazed at how soft they are, and I don't like it. It's like touching a marshmallow, and that's not

sexual to me. For me, sex is so bound up with a man, and
the feel of a man, that it's very jarring to touch a woman.
They just don't feel right at all. They're much softer than
they look, especially if they don't work out with weights. It's
almost like . . . I don't know. It doesn't work for me. Basically, I've tried everything that I've wanted to try. I wanted
to explore, and I'm not sorry I did.

"When I'm a little old lady, rocking back and forth in my
rocking chair, I hope to look back on these things fondly,
and think, yes, those were interesting, neat things to do, and
be glad I did them.

"Sometimes also, I get a very holy feeling during sex. A
sense of oneness, of integrity, feeling that it is so right. At
these times, I wonder how sex became so debased, so much
a subject of negative thinking. To me, sex contains a medley
of feelings. It's perfectly all right if sex is a great symphony
orchestra. I've had those ethereal experiences, but sex can
also be a quick ragtime band, or a humming of a melody,
and there's nothing wrong with that. It can be all those
things, depending on what you need, and where you are at
the time. I guess my feeling is you should let sex be what it
is, when it is. And if you're looking only for symphony or-
chestras or heavenly bands, you are going to miss so much.
And I really don't want to miss any of it. Just because sex is
not all heavenly choir singing doesn't mean that it's not
worthwhile and valid. I think I'd get tired of only heavenly
choirs.

"Sometimes sex is like another experience I've had, kind
of an out-of-body experience. The first time was when I had
been married for maybe a year, and it was beyond sex. I've
had that same kind of experience since then, but it doesn't

seem to occur with any kind of predictability. But when it does, it's as if at one time, I feel a kinship with the tiniest grain of sand, or even smaller, the infinitesimal. As if I take in all of infinity. It's not an experience that lasts very long. It's as if it becomes troubling to be out of myself, and I go back to myself. But at the time, at least briefly, it's very pleasant."

At this point Helen paused. It was clear that we needed a break, some food, and a chance to unwind. We ordered seared Ahi salads, a house specialty.

Despite the implications of these disclosures, Helen had been amazingly candid in describing her sexual history. She had done things that many people only fantasize about. She had had sex with a woman, with two men at the same time, with a man and woman simultaneously, and she had attended (though not actively participated in) a full-out orgy. But always she seemed to be doing it to please her partner. The *ménage à trois* with the fashion model, for example, was orchestrated for Oliver's sake, as was the episode with the Mexican diplomat. The one time she experimented with another woman to satisfy her own curiosity, she found it rather distasteful.

Helen, it appears, is what is known as "behaviorally bisexual." That is, she is a heterosexual woman who has, on occasion, had sex with other women. In contrast, many women (and men) are truly bisexual: they are sexually attracted to both sexes. And though such individuals may establish love relationships with only one sex, their erotic interests are fluid and are not limited to the neatly organized categories of heterosexual and homosexual. However, as my co-author, Steve Pinkerton, and I discuss at length in our book *With Pleasure*, not all sex is motivated by erotic desire. In Helen's case her bisexuality appears to have been driven mainly by an urge to please her (male) partner, as well as a desire for sexual adventure and self-exploration.

"I really think we can get past this," she began again. "I believe that healing is possible for all the pains that people feel, all of the horrors that are visited upon us as children. As adults we can serve as our own parents. We can look at our needs, and be a guide for ourselves. To go back and help ourselves look again at what happened to us, and guide us toward a healthier way of looking at things. I know that I've experienced that—you don't have to be a victim forever. I know that I've healed myself, and that I've let other people heal me many times. It can happen, and that's why I believe that Katie and I can have a healthy life, in spite of this horror. I'm so glad that there have been people who have believed in me. It is hard to believe in yourself when others don't. But now I realize that no matter what they do to me, they can't make these accusations true. They can't make me guilty of any of those things. Those things did not happen, and they can't make them happen."

After a pregnant pause, I did my best to reassure her that the courts would eventually see her case for what it was, and she would be exonerated. (I'm not sure she believed this any more than I did.)

Throughout our conversation I found myself marveling at her intelligence and openness, and at her obvious love for her daughter. Her candor—particularly with regard to her sexual history—was especially refreshing, even surprising, in light of her precarious legal circumstances (remember, this is a woman whose sexual behavior and values had come under intense *criminal* scrutiny). Accused of a sexual crime, Helen had every motivation to omit or alter the more sensational aspects of her sex life. Instead, Helen seemed unwilling to whitewash her sexual past or to offer apologies or excuses for the path she took. Helen had, once again, acquitted herself admirably.

After so many days of uncertainty, I was now convinced that Helen was innocent. It would have made a unique case report if she had actually sexually molested her daughter— one that the psychology journals would be unable to resist— but it was clear to me by this point that nothing of the kind had ever happened. Helen was the victim of a cruel misunderstanding, a misunderstanding that threatened to ruin her life.

We sat in silence for several minutes, then I paid the check and we headed for the car. On the drive back to Mendocino I officially offered my services to Helen, as an expert witness, a social scientist, and an ally. But I needed to interview Katherine, I informed her, and the sooner the better. I promised to call her in the next few days to arrange a time when I could begin the interviewing process.

On the plane ride home to L.A. I attempted to put the pieces together. I thought back to our earlier discussion at the Heritage House and to Helen's passion for sex, for love, and for life. Like the young woman featured in my book, *Sarah: A*

Sexual Biography, Helen's passion for sex is suffused with spiritual and religious overtones. A very deep spiritualism seems to pervade her life experiences, sexual and otherwise. Though one might expect to find such emotions in religiously devout individuals, Helen is not especially faithful. Anyway, sex and religion make strange bedfellows even under the best of circumstances. Clearly, Helen is searching for the deeper meaning in life's many turns. Her most profound relationships were based on sex, it seems, so it is not surprising that she should seek the spiritual in bed.

But perhaps this spiritualism is merely window dressing, designed to lend the illusion of substance to her sexual escapades. Maybe Helen wraps her sexual experiences in a soul-searching disguise to elevate them beyond the mundane, the potentially perverse. Similar excuses are proffered by some drug abusers, who claim to be seeking God through chemically induced changes to their neurophysiology. In Helen's case, however, she makes no excuses for her behavior, normative or not. Some experiences she liked, some she didn't. Some she initiated for her own benefit, some for the benefit of others. In all cases, however, she takes full responsibility for her actions. Believing, or certainly hoping that when she looks back on her life, she will experience it as a life fully lived.

Similarly, she does not imply that her sexual escapades were driven by spiritual forces. Instead, they were motivated by her need for a rich and varied emotional life. And, while one could certainly question her approach to emotional intimacy—given her inability to sustain a long-term relationship and her penchant for sexual diversity over sexual stability—Helen never resorts to defending her behavior as part of her quest for God. The spiritual or reverent feelings that she reports having during sex seem spontaneous, not calculated, for either my benefit or hers.

A FEW DAYS WITH KATHERINE

Two weeks later I was back in northern California, staying at my "second home," the MacCallum House. I had arranged to spend several days in Mendocino with the goal of building rapport with Katherine so that she would feel comfortable talking to me. I was hoping to get her side of the story and, especially, to gain some insight into why she had seemingly changed her story after the initial interview by Child Protective Services. I also wanted to get a better sense of her personality, her mental abilities, and her overall psychological makeup. The information I gathered wouldn't be official (the "official," court-ordered psychological evaluation had been conducted by another psychologist weeks before), but it would help me assist Helen prepare her case.

I spent a total of four days with Helen and Katherine during this trip to Mendocino, but the primary concern, Katherine's sexual behavior, was not discussed until the last several hours of the visit. The first few days were devoted to rapport building and consisted of fun activities in which all three of us could participate. The first day, we paddled a canoe around the inlet to the bay, below the Mendicino bluffs, and on the second day we went horseback riding—a two-

hour trail ride through the coastal forests, stopping for a picnic lunch on a rugged mountain top. Katherine, it turned
out, was enamored with horses, as are many girls her age.
On the third day, we took an old-time "skunk" train ride
east to Willits. (The derivation of "skunk" quickly became
apparent as the stench of burning fuel filled our nostrils.)
Odor notwithstanding, we had a very pleasant ride through
the redwood forest. Once again, a picnic lunch was served at
the midpoint of our journey.

On the fourth day, Katherine and I (without Helen) went
to Wild Adventures, a nearby wild animal park. It was the
kind of place where the animals roam, but the people don't.
Humans ride in safari vehicles through fields scattered with
buffalo, elk, big-horn sheep, moose, and zebra. Katherine
liked the zebras best and vowed someday to have one as a
pet.

After the "safari," we lunched together on a grassy knoll,
overlooking a bird sanctuary. This was my first chance to
talk to Katherine alone. After the previous three days of casual discussions and easy interactions, however, it seemed
perfectly natural to Katherine that we should spend part of
the day alone together. A more formal interview evolved,
rather naturally, out of a discussion about school, and art
activities in particular. Katherine was describing finger-
painting, and how, if you re-wet the paintings, you can re-
fashion them. She mentioned that "mommy and I do that at
home."

I seized this opportunity (using a soft, but direct voice) to
ask Katherine if she had any idea why they took her away
from her mother's home. She replied, "No. My mom didn't
do anything. They thought my mommy touched me in my

private place, but she didn't. And I had to stay away for five days, with a different family. That family wouldn't even let me cry. They kept telling me I had to stop. They yelled at me."

Noting that Katherine used the words "private place" instead of "vagina," I wanted to see if she would use the word "vagina" in another context. I took out a small picture book that I had been dutifully carrying around in my jacket pocket for the last three days. The book contained drawings that described babies and childbirth in a way that children could understand. Although Katherine was at first hesitant to discuss the pictures, she soon warmed up, and began to initiate conversations about the different scenarios depicted in the drawings. As her comments made clear, Katherine was well versed in the correct usage of anatomical terms. At no time, however, did it appear that Katherine's knowledge about sexuality exceeded her developmental stage. Her knowledge was consistent with a didactic exposure to the structure of the genitals, secondary sex characteristics (e.g., breasts for nursing), and basic reproductive functions.

In contrast, the police and Child Protective Services seemed to believe that Katherine's usage of anatomically correct terms indicated that she was "over-sexualized." That is, they thought she knew too much about sex, which they interpreted as a consequence of having been sexually molested by her mother.

To test this hypothesis, I showed Katherine a series of photographs of fertility symbols, and asked her to describe what she saw. Her responses were very naive. When I showed her a picture of a clay Peruvian statue of a short, squat man with a very large erection, for example, she told

me she saw "a man riding a camel." She clearly had no con-
ception of sexual functions per se, let alone of sexual arousal
and intercourse. Her knowledge was limited to a cursory—
but correct—familiarity with human anatomy.

Next, I set up a series of simple experiments to test her
use of the words "in" and "on." The police report indicted
that, according to Katherine, Helen had put something *in*
Katherine's vagina. The goal of my experiments was to dis-
cern what Katherine really meant by "in." In the course of
these tests I asked her to do several tasks, including con-
structing or completing sentences that required correctly using "in" and "on," and a picture-sorting task that required
knowing the distinction between these two words. The results of these experiments suggested that Katherine used the
words interchangeably, often mistakenly using "in" when
she clearly meant "on," and vice versa. Thus, the inconsistencies between Helen's story and the police report could
easily have been caused by a little girl's inability to distinguish between two similar prepositions.

I showed Katherine a group of nonprescription medicines, including a bottle of Pepto-Bismol, a bottle of aspirin,
a tube of Neosporin, and a sheet of allergy pills. When
asked, she described each and every one of them as "medicine." Significantly, she also picked up the Neosporin without prompting and said, "this is the medicine my mommy
put on my vagina." This time, at least, Katherine used the
correct preposition ("on"), while clearly identifying Neosporin as the medicine her mother had used on her.

Finally, when I showed her a tampon, she said, "Oh, I
know what that is. Mommy uses it in the bathroom."

"Where does mommy put it?" I asked. Although Katherine did not use the anatomically correct term, she stated, in essence, that her mother put it in her anus. This finding was significant, because, after further inquiry, it became apparent that *Katherine did not conceive of the vagina as an orifice* and therefore, if the tampon were put "in" anything, it must be the anus. Thus, despite what the police believed, Katherine couldn't possibly have meant that a dildo or other object was inserted into her vagina.

Our conversation continued during the hour-long drive back to Mendocino. After a bit of small talk about the animals we had just seen, I steered the conversation around to school and her behavior there. She admitted having masturbated and having pulled up her dress to show her panties to some of the other children, but she insisted that other children at her school did it as well. Somehow, they didn't get caught but she did, which she didn't think was fair. Then she asked why she couldn't masturbate at school and I explained to her that masturbation is a private activity that should only be done at home. Some things aren't appropriate for school, I told her. She wouldn't wear her pajamas to school, would she?

Just before we reached Mendocino, we stopped off at a "home-made" ice cream parlor, where we were joined by Helen. I told Helen that the interview had been very helpful and informative. I reassured her—wrongly, as it turned out—that once the results of the court-ordered psychological evaluation of Katherine became known, the whole incident would be dismissed. (I incorrectly assumed that the court-appointed psychologist—an expert in his own right, I thought—would elicit the same information as I had, and would arrive at the same conclusions.) Until we received copies of Katherine's psychological evaluation, all we could do was wait: Helen in Mendocino, and me in Los Angeles.

THE CLOUD DARKENS

Two days later a fax arrived for me at my office in the psychology department. It was Dr. Thomas Carrier's court-ordered evaluation of Katherine Cross. Having read dozens of these psychological reports in my time, I knew that what really matters to the courts is the bottom line. So I quickly turned to Dr. Carrier's conclusions. A deadening chill crept over me as I read the last line of his report. "And I conclude that this is definitely an indication of mother-daughter incest," he wrote. How could he have reached such a conclusion, I wondered? Had I missed something?

I tore into the body of the report, fueled by curiosity and dread. By the time I had finished reading the entire psychological evaluation, I was outraged. The "evidence" of mother-daughter incest that seemed so convincing to Dr. Carrier was limited to Katherine's refusal to discuss the incident! Dr. Carrier viewed her reticence as an indication that she was hiding a deep, dark secret, which he thought *must* be mother-daughter incest. Upon rereading his conclusions, I found myself dazed and incredulous. Since when was failure to communicate evidence of a crime? Given Katherine's age and the fact that she had been bombarded by police officers, doctors, Child Protective Service workers, and teachers—not to mention being torn from her mother and placed in a foster home—her reluctance to talk to yet another person about this incident seemed completely understandable.

Adding insult to injury, I noted that in the two-hour evaluation period, Katherine was subjected to five psychological tests, including an I.Q. test, the Thematic Apperception Test (which consists of pictures of scenes about which the test-taker is asked to make up an appropriate story), a draw-a-person test, and so forth. A conservative estimate of the time necessary to administer these tests (which, incidentally, were not given by Dr. Carrier but by an assistant) left maybe ten or twenty minutes for discussing Katherine's sexual behavior. So, in the absence of any effort at rapport building or establishing any therapeutic relationship, Dr. Carrier had concluded that Katherine was the victim of incest, and that her mother was the guilty party. He arrived at this conclusion not only in spite of the fact that Katherine had said nothing of the kind, *but because of it*! Somehow, he interpreted her silence as a symptom of incest.

There was now a police report, a Child Protective Services report, a gynecological report, and a psychologist's report, all claiming that Helen had sexually molested her daughter, and all, it appeared to me, completely wrong. When I called Helen and summarized Dr. Carrier's findings, she was devastated. Over and over she cried, "How could he say that? How could he?" I calmed her down as best I could, but made sure she realized the seriousness of the situation. The weight of professional opinion was now completely against her. It was time, I advised her, to take aggressive action to protect herself and her daughter. To begin with, she needed to get a *real* lawyer, one with extensive experience in incest cases and a proven record of success. She needed someone like Megan Douglas.

Megan Douglas is a first-rate defense attorney with a national reputation as a tough litigator. As a former police officer and district attorney, she is especially skilled at dismantling investigation foibles. She knows the ropes, and never backs off. In the courtroom she looks, and acts, like she's in control—with one hand pointing and the other resting on her hip. To add to her legal clout, she is also a cousin of former Supreme Court Justice William Douglas (in the law, family ties still matter).

Megan and I had previously worked together on several occasions. She seemed perfect for this case. My only fear was that she had moved up in the ranks, so to speak. Word was out that she was due to be nominated to the Superior Court bench. Though I really like Megan and under normal circumstances would wish her every success, in this instance I selfishly hoped that the rumors were false.

Luckily, Megan was available and had the time to litigate a case in Mendocino County. She was not inexpensive, however. Soon after Megan had agreed to take the case, Helen cashed in her assets, starting with her Jack White stock and mutual funds accounts. She also made a discrete call to an old friend (Oliver, actually), and established a line of credit.

ABRAMSON'S REPORT

A very disturbing scenario was being played out in the Helen Cross case. If Katherine were taken away from Helen, she would probably spend the rest of her childhood in a series of foster homes, denied the love of her natural mother. This happy little five-year-old would be changed and likely scarred forever. The impact on Helen also would be devastating. Katherine was her life. But none of this seemed to matter. For whatever reason, the powers that be were now determined to convict Helen Cross of sexually molesting her daughter.

Megan and I couldn't let that happen. We met in San Francisco to strategize. The next step, we decided, was for me to summarize my findings about the case into a report. Perhaps the report, which addressed the substance of Helen's and Katherine's comments during our lengthy interviews, could derail the momentum toward trial. Something was needed to slow things down and to get the evidence reevaluated. We hoped my report would do the trick.

I submitted the report to the Court, the District Attorney's Office, Julia Escobar (Katherine's attorney), and to Child Protective Services. Here's what I sent them:

PSYCHOLOGICAL EVALUATION

CLIENT NAME(S): Cross, Helen (mother) and Cross, Katherine (daughter)

DATE OF REPORT: August 11, 1997

REFERRAL: I was contacted by Helen Cross on July 12, 1997.

She had been referred to me by Margaret Schultz, a clinical psychologist at UC Berkeley.

Helen stated that she was the victim of a wrongful arrest and was accused of committing incest with her daughter, Katherine. Helen discussed her case for 20 minutes. I took her phone number and address.

I neither believed, nor disbelieved Helen's story. I called her back because I thought the case would be significant—and very unusual—regardless of its outcome. Overt mother-daughter incest is a rare occurrence. A bona fide case would be very important for my research and teaching in the area of sexual abuse. On the other hand, if Helen's story was true, a wrongful arrest for incest can have myriad psychological and cultural implications, an examination of which would also be significant. Consequently, I undertook a series of interviews with Helen and her daughter, Katherine. They were seen individually and jointly. I also asked Helen to provide me with copies of all records and testimony, including those that supported her case and those that were contrary to her position. In light of the significance of this case and its value for research, Helen was charged no fees.

ASSESSMENT METHOD: Interview, for both mother and daughter. Anatomical drawings; descriptions of sculpture; and object definitions were used with the daughter.

EVALUATION OF KATHERINE CROSS (DAUGHTER): Katherine was seen over the course of several days. She is an alert, attractive, 5-year-old girl, with blond hair and light complexion.

The first few days were used to build rapport. Katherine was attentive, but reserved. To ease the tension, we discussed horses and other animals, her favorite television

shows, and the things she liked to do with her friends. Later
we had a simple, but animated talk about school and about
art.

During the clinical interview, Katherine was initially reticent to discuss anything sexual, quickly changing the subject. She appeared nervous and confused and avoided eye
contact with me. To shift the burden of explanation away
from her, I introduced a book on pregnancy and childbirth.
Together we examined the anatomical drawings and photographs. Katherine enjoyed the book, and participated by
bringing herself closer to me, and by turning the pages. She
talked animatedly about the external changes in a pregnant
woman's body, plus the variations in the size and position
of the fetus. However, when asked to name the external female genitals, Katherine replied, "I don't know." Because
Helen Cross had previously told me that Katherine knew the
word "vagina," I continued the conversation using the correct anatomical terms. Eventually, Katherine did the same
and we had a lengthy conversation about rudimentary concepts of pregnancy and birth.

When the interview continued, Katherine seemed much
more comfortable in my presence and spoke openly about
sexuality and her own behavior. She acknowledged masturbating at school, but felt that she was being singled out for
punishment. Other children were also doing it, she claimed,
but experienced no retribution. In her eyes, she was just a
scapegoat.

I talked with Katherine about discrimination learning—
about how some behaviors were only appropriate in certain
situations, and at particular places. There was a proper
place for masturbation, and it wasn't at school, it was at

home, in private. She asked, "What about when I'm in school, in private?" I told her that she knew the answer, which was that masturbation at school was always inappropriate. She nodded.

I also tested Katherine's general knowledge of sexual anatomy and functioning. Although she has a rudimentary grasp of terms and appearance, she has a very limited knowledge of function. She has no concept of the vagina as an orifice (which is appropriate for her age). When shown a tampon, she told me she knew exactly what it was, and she said her "mommy uses it in the bathroom." When I asked her where her mother inserts it, she told me in the anus. I showed Katherine a photograph of a Peruvian sculpture depicting a man with a large erection and asked her to tell me what it was. She told me it was a man riding a camel.

In contrast to her limited sexual knowledge, she correctly identified several over-the-counter medicines as "diarrhea medicine," "eye drops," "pills," and so forth, but she didn't know the specific brand or generic name. She knew it was diarrhea medicine, but not Pepto-Bismol; she identified "white medicine pills," but did not know it was aspirin. In each instance, I believe that Katherine was responding truthfully. Sexuality questions were never isolated from other questions, and she responded to both in the same manner (especially after she became comfortable and began to trust me). Some things she identified correctly, others not.

Katherine is a very bright, very extroverted, curious little girl. She is aware that she implicated her mother by saying that her mother touched her vagina, but I firmly believe that she made the remark to legitimize her own masturbation. In all subsequent interviews, she has denied that her mother has ever touched her vagina. I believe this to be true—at least in reference to sexual molestation. Also, as Katherine has no concept of the vagina as an orifice, I do not believe that she ever said (or meant to imply) that her mother put anything *in* her vagina. Furthermore, Katherine freely admits that her mother put medication *on* her vagina, and states that this is the only contact her mother had with her vagina. Although Katherine is aware that her comments were related to her being removed from the home, I do not believe that her retraction is based on pressure from her mother. Katherine eventually talked very openly in my presence about all aspects of her sexuality, including behavior that would get her in trouble (masturbation and sexual play at school), and freely answered questions she did not anticipate (e.g., the use of a tampon).

EVALUATION OF HELEN CROSS (MOTHER): Helen is a 43-year-old, single mother with a Ph.D. in electrical engineering from Stanford University. I found her to be open, cooperative, and nondefensive. Although distraught and needing acceptance, she did not seem manipulative, coercive, pleading, or obsequious. Helen realized that my conclusions could either support or cast aspersions on her story. However, she made no attempt to praise herself, flatter me, or elicit my sympathy.

In light of the circumstances, Helen's emotional responses appear genuine. She obviously takes this matter seriously, which was conveyed in all of her gestures (i.e., manner of speaking, eye contact, etc.). This is an emotionally charged time for her. However, she spent little effort protesting her innocence. Instead, she presented her side of the story, which I believe rings true. That is, Katherine was talking about (or elaborating upon) the application of medication for a vaginal irritation.

A large portion of the clinical interview with Helen focused on potential defensiveness and denial. I found little evidence of either. Helen openly discussed her limitations and assets as a person and as a mother. She readily admitted her past mistakes and made no attempt to idealize her parenting skills. She openly discussed her sexual relationships, her family background, and her achievements and struggles. I believe that she was being honest, to the best of her ability.

Other observations support this conclusion. Parents who are hiding a family secret do not put their children in therapy. Over time, children establish a close bond with a therapist and often will freely betray family secrets. Given Helen's sophistication, she is no doubt well aware of this possibility. However, Katherine was in therapy for months prior to the main incident at the school.

In conclusion, I believe that Helen is a knowledgeable, caring mother who has never had inappropriate sexual contact with her daughter.

SUMMARY: In summation, I found no evidence of sexual contact between mother and daughter. Although it is possible that Katherine has been sexually molested by *someone* in her environment, it is more likely that her sexual interest and behavior represent the extreme end of normal variation in childhood sexual play.

Paul R. Abramson, Ph.D.

For several days, I anxiously awaited reactions to my report. Although I received a perfunctory notice that the court had received the document, no comment was attached.

The first response to my report came from Julia Escobar, Katherine's court-appointed lawyer. I was delighted when she called and told me that she concurred—in every respect—with my conclusions. This was a major coup. At the very least, it reduced the number of "fronts" on which Helen, Megan, and I needed to battle. Katherine's lawyer was now in our corner.

Even more significant was the letter I received from the district attorney's office: "After careful review of Dr. Abramson's report, we have decided to drop the charges against Helen Cross." We were ecstatic! Victory was now within reach!

Unfortunately, our reach turned out to be a tad short. Completely ignoring the DA's recommendation, Child Protective Services described my report as "irrelevant" and indicated that they intended to pursue the case. They were convinced that Helen Cross was a child molester and they were going to bring her to justice. If the district attorney was unwilling to try the case, they would go over his head, to the Office of County Counsel. This CPS did. But, to their chagrin, the director of the County Counsel office also agreed with my report, and turned down Child Protective Services' request for prosecution. Undeterred, Child Protective Services appealed directly to the attorney general of the State of California. He, in turn, sent a mandate to County Counsel: prosecute Helen Cross.

THE TRIAL BEGINS

Mendocino is a quaint little town, rich in natural beauty and California history. The Pacific coastline is dramatic, the old-growth redwood forest is majestic, and the architecture is magnificent and compelling, with ornate, turn-of-the-century buildings abutting modern functional styles. Yet, beyond the daily influx of tourists who are attracted by the idyllicism of the surroundings, nothing much happens in Mendocino.

As befits a town its size, Mendocino maintains little more than a skeletal judicial system. The courthouse in which juvenile cases are heard is a trailer that is also used as an overflow classroom when the local primary school exceeds its expected enrollment. A second trailer adjoins the first and provides restrooms to courtroom visitors or students, as necessary. The headquarters of the Mendocino Sheriff's Department is located just a few hundred feet away, in yet another trailer.

At present, the courthouse is "parked" in the midst of the redwood forest, just north of the city limits. The trailer is ringed by the massive hulks of formerly towering redwood trees and the surrounding grounds are blanketed with redwood needles that fill the air with a sweet pine scent. Deep green moss hugs the trees and buildings and adds to the serene atmosphere of this locale.

The courtroom itself is exceedingly small and claustrophobic. A raised platform serves as the judge's bench. Tiny tables, facing the judge, are used for attorney workspace. The court reporter sits to one side of the platform and the witness sits to the other. A total of eight chairs, strewn about the remaining space, constitute the courtroom gallery. Behind the platform is the judge's chamber, which is little more than a furnished closet containing a small desk, a black leather chair, and a book shelf. Visitors to the chamber must stand before the judge, because there are no other chairs.

The cramped quarters of this courtroom have a confrontational effect on the proceedings, bringing foes—prosecution and defense—literally face to face with one another. When tempers flare and tears flow, as they invariably do, there is nowhere to hide. As a consequence, the tension is often palpable in the overcrowded Mendocino County courthouse, especially in highly contested cases, such as Helen Cross's.

The trial itself was a gut-wrenching experience for everyone involved. The stakes were high and Helen had much to lose. If the judge found sufficient evidence of molestation, he could recommend criminal proceedings, and Helen could go to jail. Worse, she could lose custody of her daughter, forever.

ABRAMSON'S TESTIMONY

There were ten people (including myself) in the tiny courtroom when the trial began Thursday morning on September 7, a typically drizzly, overcast, Pacific-coast day. Helen was joined by her attorney, Megan Douglas, while Katherine (who was not present) was represented by her own attorney, Julia Escobar. The prosecution included Dave Monk, the attorney from County Counsel, and the two social workers from Child Protective Services, Matt Bickel and Marcia Osborn. The court was presided over by the Honorable Donald Shriver. A court reporter, Jeanna Schmidt, recorded the proceedings. The following notes are drawn directly from her transcriptions.

After preliminary motions had been dispensed with, Helen's attorney reminded Judge Shriver "that the Department's counsel, Mr. Monk, [had] agreed to take Dr. Paul Abramson out of order, and allow us to have him testify first, so that he can sit in on the rest of the proceedings." Monk confirmed that he had agreed to this arrangement, and after Julia had granted her assent as well, I was called to the stand to testify.

The primary reason that I was asked to testify out of order is that I hoped to write a book (this book!) about the case and I felt that I needed to be present throughout the entire proceeding in order to detect important nuances in testimony and participate in off-the-record discussions. Naturally, Helen was supportive of my research objectives (especially since I was providing my expertise *pro bono*), as was her attorney, Megan. However, I also needed to obtain the prosecutor's approval. This he granted, with one proviso, that I testify first. The advantage to Monk was that he could better challenge my testimony if it was heard before his witnesses testified. Normally, the prosecution must present its case first. Thus, by giving me permission to sit throughout the proceedings and having me testify at the beginning, Monk could potentially gain a strategic advantage. On the other hand, Megan was convinced that the order of my testimony was inconsequential. So, she felt that she was giving nothing away.

Before I could begin my testimony in the Cross case, the judge asked Monk if he wanted to conduct a *voir dire* examination of my qualifications. (*Voir dire* examinations are used to resolve issues that must be decided before the trial can continue.) Since I was to testify as an expert witness in this case, Monk accepted the opportunity to question my expertise. What follows is Monk's examination:

Mr. Monk: Dr. Abramson, you have a Ph.D. in psychology?

Dr. Abramson: Yes, I do.

Mr. Monk: Are you a licensed clinical psychologist?

Dr. Abramson: No, I am not.

Mr. Monk: Without a license, are you qualified to use psychological tests?

Dr. Abramson: Although I do not administer psychological tests as part of my expert-witness work, I do administer and interpret them for teaching and research purposes. I have published research on psychological tests and have served on the editorial board of the leading journal devoted to personality assessment. I have also authored a textbook on personality psychology that devotes considerable attention to the administration, evaluation, validity, and reliability of psychological tests.

Although he had asked only three questions, Monk's strategy was readily apparent—he hoped to convince the judge that my lack of a clinical license should disqualify me as an expert witness in this case. This is not an uncommon strategy for attorneys to use in challenging the qualifications of the other side's expert witnesses. However, it is often difficult to get a judge to dismiss an expert, particularly someone like me, who has been "qualified" as an expert before, is a professor at a major university, and has published widely on the subject under consideration. Even if this strategy fails, the attorney hopes his or her questioning will make the expert feel nervous or inadequate and thereby adversely affect the witness' performance on the stand. An ineffective witness is little better than a disqualified one, and could even be a liability to his or her side.

However, the attorney must be careful about the manner in which he or she challenges the expert's qualifications. If the attorney appears unreasonable, or mean-spirited, or the judge feels that the attorney is badgering the witness, it can work against him or her, particularly if the prospective witness is obviously an expert in his or her field. The attorney also risks antagonizing and energizing the witness to respond to the courtroom challenge with renewed motivation to do his or her best.

Mr. Monk: So, am I to understand that you do not administer standard psychological tests?

Dr. Abramson: That is correct.

Mr. Monk: Is that because you can not?

Dr. Abramson: I believe I responded to that already. I have administered literally hundreds—probably thousands—of psychology tests for teaching and research purposes.

Mr. Monk: Don't you need a psychology licence to do that?

Ms. Douglas: Objection. Asked and answered.

The Court (Judge Shriver): Sustained.

Mr. Monk: Your Honor, I have no further questions of this witness.

With this, Monk concluded his *voir dire* examination of whether I was qualified to be an expert witness in this case. He had tried, and ultimately failed, to argue that I could not be an expert because I am not a licensed psychotherapist.

It was now Megan's turn to begin qualifying me as her expert. Her intent was to ask me questions that would allow me to highlight my competence and substantial experience in the area of sexual abuse in order to convince Judge Shriver that I should be allowed to testify in the Cross case.

Ms. Douglas: Dr. Abramson, where are you presently employed?

Dr. Abramson: I am a professor of psychology at UCLA—the University of California at Los Angeles.

Ms. Douglas: How long have you been there?

Dr. Abramson: This is my twenty-first year.

Ms. Douglas: And what courses are you teaching at present?

Dr. Abramson: I teach courses on personality, human sexuality, and sex and the law.

Ms. Douglas: And what is your educational background?

Dr. Abramson: I have a bachelor's degree, a master's degree, and a Ph.D. in psychology.

Ms. Douglas: As a psychologist, have you had any experiences dealing with cases of incest or sexual molestation?

Dr. Abramson: Yes, I have.

Ms. Douglas: Can you tell us the extent of that experience?

Dr. Abramson: I have worked on a large number of criminal and civil cases involving sexual molestation—primarily from the prosecution and plaintiff sides—though, on occasion, I have also done defense work. I have also worked for several of the district attorneys' offices throughout southern California, and have worked for many of the prominent "personal injury" law firms on the civil side of these types of cases.

Ms. Douglas: Can you also give us an estimate of the number of alleged sexual molestation victims you have interviewed?

Dr. Abramson: Over 100. And as the Court is probably aware, I have also written a book on one such case, titled *Sarah: A Sexual Biography.*

Ms. Douglas: You say that you are usually an expert witness for the prosecution. Is that correct?

Dr. Abramson: That is correct.

Ms. Douglas: And can you give us an estimate of how many times you have been engaged by the prosecution in a case to act as their expert?

Dr. Abramson: At least 30 times.

Ms. Douglas: Did you, in fact, testify in those other cases?

Dr. Abramson: Not in all. Often, after writing my report, the defendant pled guilty.

Ms. Douglas: Attached to your report, which the Court has seen but not accepted into evidence, is your resume. It is 16 pages long, and contains 85 publications, including 6 books. It also lists about 60 talks to professional organizations or universities. Is this an accurate characterization?

Dr. Abramson: Yes, it is.

Ms. Douglas: No further questions on the issue of the witness' qualifications, Your Honor.

The Court: Mr. Monk?

Mr. Monk: No, Your Honor.

The Court: It is obvious that Dr. Abramson has enormous experience in this field and the Court will allow him to testify.

With this formality over, Megan was permitted to use my testimony to defend Helen. Her first line of questioning concerned my evaluation of Katherine. I had spent quite a bit of time with Katherine in order to earn her trust so that she would speak openly and honestly with me. This was a key point that Megan would do her best to hammer home during my testimony. Later, when the court-appointed psychologist, Dr. Carrier, testified, Megan would highlight how little time he had spent with Katherine and how this might have affected the validity of that interview. In contrast, the rapport I had established with Katherine permitted me to delve deeper into her psyche and to try to understand why she had apparently contradicted herself when talking to the authorities.

The Court: Ms. Douglas, you may begin your direct examination of Dr. Abramson.

Ms. Douglas: Thank you, Your Honor. Dr. Abramson, did you interview the daughter, Katherine Cross?

Dr. Abramson: Yes, I did.

Ms. Douglas: And can you tell us the total time that you spent interviewing her?

Dr. Abramson: Including rapport building, I spent four days with her—either alone or with her mother present.

Ms. Douglas: Dr. Abramson, when you interviewed Katherine Cross, was her mother there?

Dr. Abramson: Not for the "clinical interview."

Ms. Douglas: But she was present during your other interviews with Katherine?

Dr. Abramson: Yes. I spent quite a bit of time with both Helen and Katherine in order to build rapport.

Ms. Douglas: What did you do during this time?

Dr. Abramson: We rode horses, went for a train ride, canoed, went to McDonald's and Katherine's other favorite places to eat, and so forth. Basically, we did things that she wanted to do.

Ms. Douglas: And what was the point of these activities?

Dr. Abramson: I wanted Katherine to feel comfortable with me. People in general, and kids especially, need to trust you before they'll discuss intimate details of their lives.

Ms. Douglas: And were you successful?

Dr. Abramson: I think so. For example, when I first asked her questions relating to sexuality, she was obviously uncomfortable and tried to change the subject. Instead of pursuing it further, we played a game. I have a Rolodex with a few fake numbers in it, and she played with that. When she found the telephone number for a tooth fairy recording, she asked me to call it on my cellular phone. We continued to talk and played games, until I thought she felt less pressured.

Ms. Douglas: Was her attitude different during what you have called the "clinical interview"?

Dr. Abramson: Very much. She seemed comfortable in my presence and was interested in talking. I showed her some books and pictures that deal with human sexuality in a very simplified way. I used these as a vehicle for talking with her about pregnancy and birth. The ultimate purpose was to get her to feel comfortable, so that I could ask her questions about sex, as well as questions about possible incest and sexual molestation.

Ms. Douglas: Was she more comfortable talking about those subjects?

Dr. Abramson: Yes, she was very comfortable then and didn't seem to mind talking about sex.

Ms. Douglas: Did you have an opportunity to discuss whether she saw the vagina as an orifice—a space that one could put something into?

Dr. Abramson: Yes. It was very important for me to make that assessment. I had read a previous report which indicated that Katherine said that something was inserted into her vagina. Because I have published research on children's attitudes and beliefs about sexuality, I was aware that many young girls don't conceive of the vagina as an orifice—in large part, because of the intact hymen. They know where urine comes from, and they are aware of the possibility of pleasurable sensations from the vaginal region. Yet, they don't conceive of it as an orifice. Therefore, I was interested to see if Katherine did. So, I set up a series of tests to examine her knowledge of some basic sexual "facts." In one, I showed her a tampon and asked her to identify it. Katherine said she knew what it was: "Mommy uses it in the bathroom." I asked her what her mommy does with it, and she replied, "Mommy puts it inside her" and indicated that it was inserted in the anus, although she didn't use that particular term. At other times, Katherine indicated that the vagina is just a surface structure, not an orifice. As I mentioned, this is a common belief among young girls.

Ms. Douglas: Did you have the opportunity to discuss with Katherine her removal from her mother's home?

Dr. Abramson: Yes, I did.

Ms. Douglas: And what was her reaction to that event?

Dr. Abramson: She was severely traumatized by it and she was still very frightened. Katherine and Helen have an enormously close bond. I observed this throughout my interviews with them. Katherine also made comments about her closeness and love for her mother. For Katherine, this was one of the most disruptive things she could imagine.

Ms. Douglas: During this discussion about her removal from the home, did you question Katherine as to why she was removed?

Dr. Abramson: Yes, I did. She indicated that she had said some things that were misinterpreted. And because of those comments, she was taken from the home.

Ms. Douglas: Did she tell you what those comments were?

Dr. Abramson: She said that her words implied that her mommy did something bad to her—touched her vagina. Which, Katherine said, "Mommy never did."

Ms. Douglas: Did you question her as to why she told someone a statement that wasn't true?

Dr. Abramson: Yes, I did.

Ms. Douglas: And her response?

Dr. Abramson: She said she was nervous, and she didn't
know how it would be interpreted.

Ms. Douglas: Doctor, in your work with children—and given
your extensive educational and research background—is it
normal for children of Katherine's age to masturbate?

Dr. Abramson: Yes, it is.

Ms. Douglas: And is it normal for children to feel that masturbation is "bad"?

Dr. Abramson: Yes and no. It depends upon cultural attitudes about sex. In some cultures, Norway for example, the
answer is no—masturbation is not normally considered
"bad." In other cultures, it is. The same is true for different
families or social environments. Yes in some, no in others.

Ms. Douglas: Is there a normal amount of masturbation for a
child of this age?

Dr. Abramson: There really aren't any good data on this issue. Most of the research on masturbation in young children
concerns the onset of masturbation. For example, it's been
observed in infants. However, the frequency of masturbation
for this age group, and older kids as well, is difficult to document, for the obvious reason that kids and parents are
usually uncomfortable with questions about masturbation.

Ms. Douglas: You have read the school reports about
Katherine acting out sexually?

Dr. Abramson: Yes.

Ms. Douglas: What is your opinion as to whether that falls within the normal levels?

Dr. Abramson: In my opinion, it falls within the normal range.

Katherine's sexual behavior ("acting out") primarily consisted of masturbation and sex play with other children. Childhood masturbation and sex play (e.g., "playing doctor") are widely recognized as nearly universal phenomena. Many preschoolers engage in genital touching or fondling, self-stimulation, and exhibitionist and voyeuristic activities. In one recent survey, nearly half of the mothers of two to five-year-old girls reported that their daughters occasionally touch their "private parts." Childhood masturbation is no longer considered problematic, as long as it is not done excessively or in inappropriate places (such as school). I did not feel that Katherine masturbated excessively, but I was concerned that she chose to express this behavior in inappropriate circumstances.

Most children begin to masturbate while still infants, and by age three or four have learned to associate the physical act of masturbation with the pleasurable sensations that accompany it. Young girls typically masturbate by rubbing or pressing their thighs together. Direct manual stimulation is less common: only 16% of the mothers in the aforementioned study reported that their daughters masturbated using their hands, and 3% stated that their children sometimes put objects into their vaginal or anal cavities.

Some children, like adults, masturbate as a means of releasing anxiety or tension. Childhood masturbation has been linked to stressful life events such as parental divorce or the birth of a sibling. In other cases, female masturbation may begin as an initial reaction to vaginal irritation, wherein rubbing or pressure on the vulva brings temporary relief, which is later recognized as pleasure. In one study, frequent masturbation was associated with disturbed parent-child relationships characterized by emotional distancing and reduced tactile contact between the parent and child. Paradoxically, it was possible that removing Katherine from her home—as would occur if Helen were found guilty—might inadvertently cause an increase in sexual misbehaviors.

Ms. Douglas: If Katherine was once again removed from her mother's home, what effect do you think it would have on her?

Dr. Abramson: I believe that Katherine would be severely traumatized because it would disrupt a very close mother-daughter bond. In fact, it could be the most disruptive influence in her life.

Ms. Douglas: Could it have any permanent effect on her?

Dr. Abramson: Yes, it could.

Ms. Douglas: And could you give us an opinion of what those permanent effects might be?

Dr. Abramson: When you take a child away from a parent— particularly a parent with whom the child has a very close, intimate relationship—you severely traumatize that child. That child loses his or her most cherished and loving relationship. This is a substantial and enduring loss. The child develops difficulty with trust, since this parent is also part of the primary trust relationship. The child also loses support, and suffers in the areas of confidence and self-esteem. And in Katherine's case, she has already been traumatized in this area. To remove her again would be devastating. Katherine now believes that she has been, once and for all, reunited with her mother—and that it was a horrendous mistake which precipitated her removal. To take her away again would be very traumatic—severely undermining her sense of security and stability.

Ms. Douglas: Could this affect her in later life?

Dr. Abramson: Definitely.

Ms. Douglas: When a child of Katherine's age is put into therapy, does the child usually develop a close relationship with her therapist?

Dr. Abramson: Yes, a child can develop very strong rapport with his or her therapist.

Ms. Douglas: And if a child has a secret—or something that the child has been told to keep secret—will it come out in a close therapeutic relationship?

Dr. Abramson: Yes, often it will. And in fact, this is one of the "values" of therapy for children. The child establishes a close, intimate bond with a non-family member who, ideally, can gain insight into the child and influence his or her development.

What Megan was attempting to establish, using me as the conduit, is the value of a successful therapeutic relationship. A child who becomes attached to a therapist will disclose everything and anything. Thus, a parent who has something to hide usually will desperately avoid therapy for his or her child. Because Helen willingly placed Katherine in therapy, my answers to these questions indirectly supported Helen's position that she did nothing to harm her child, since she apparently had nothing to hide from a therapist.

Ms. Douglas: Doctor, have you done research examining cases of mother-daughter incest? And if so, what have you found as to the frequency of mother-daughter incest?

Dr. Abramson: Yes, I have done research in this area, and I have not found a single bona fide case of mother-daughter incest where the mother was not psychotic or emotionally disturbed, or the incest was not financially motivated. Child pornography would fall into the latter category. For example, I did find one case in Georgia where the motivation was child pornography. This mother was not psychotic, at least in the usual sense of the word. She was sexually involved with her teenage daughter for financial gain. She and her husband sold the pictures through a private network.

Ms. Douglas: So, all the cases you have found have either been financially motivated or involved a psychotic or emotionally disturbed mother?

Dr. Abramson: Yes, according to my reading of the available literature. This does not mean that other cases do not exist, only that they are rare and very difficult to document. Obviously, it is possible for a mother to be the initiator of mother-daughter incest, but it appears to be extremely rare when the mother is not psychologically disturbed.

With this line of questioning, Megan Douglas was hoping to make the judge doubt the likelihood of Helen having committed incest with her five-year-old daughter by pointing out how uncommon an occurrence mother-daughter incest is. This is what is known as a "base rate argument": If pink elephants are extremely rare, how likely is it that your friend really saw one, as he adamantly claims? Mother-daughter incest is like a pink elephant, *except* when the mother is psychotic or otherwise psychologically disturbed. Megan's next task was to establish that this description did not fit Helen and therefore that the base rate argument applied.

Ms. Douglas: Doctor, did you interview Helen Cross?

Dr. Abramson: Yes I did—six or seven times, at least. At UCLA and in Mendocino.

Ms. Douglas: Did you find anything in your interview to indicate that Helen Cross was psychotic?

Dr. Abramson: No, I did not. She seemed well-grounded in reality. And she was very successful in her work and social relations. Overall, I found her to be open and nondefensive.

Ms. Douglas: Have you reviewed the Child Protective Services report in this case?

Dr. Abramson: Yes I have.

Ms. Douglas: Did you read police reports?

Dr. Abramson: Yes I did.

Ms. Douglas: Did you read anything in those documents that would tend to indicate that Helen Cross was psychotic?

Dr. Abramson: No, I didn't.

Ms. Douglas: What is your opinion as to the psychological makeup of Helen Cross?

Dr. Abramson: She is a distraught mother, who is very concerned about her daughter. She is also under considerable

duress. However, as I mentioned, I found her to be nondefensive about her life and her parenting—both the successes and failures.

Often, in these cases, you hear people say, "I am innocent. I am the best parent in the world. I only care about my
kids. I would never do this! How could you believe it?" But
from Helen, I heard both sides—the things she was proud
of, and the things that embarrassed her.

Ms. Douglas: Were any of her failures or embarrassments related to sexual contact with Katherine?

Dr. Abramson: None whatsoever.

Ms. Douglas: Dr. Abramson, having interviewed both Helen
and Katherine, do you have an opinion as to whether
Katherine Cross is the victim of sexual molestation?

Dr. Abramson: Yes, I do.

Ms. Douglas: And what is that opinion?

Dr. Abramson: First, I believe that there has never been any
sexual contact between mother and daughter. And, second,
I don't think that there is sufficient evidence to conclude
that Katherine has been molested by anyone.

Ms. Douglas: But it is still possible that Katherine was molested by someone?

Dr. Abramson: Yes, it is certainly possible. But not by her
mother.

Ms. Douglas: Thank you, Dr. Abramson.

This is an important point. Katherine's sexual behavior at
school was striking enough to draw the attention of her
teachers. It was possible, though far from certain, that this
behavior reflected premature sexualization. But there was no

indication that her mother had molested her in any fashion
or had inappropriately exposed her to sexual material.

It was then the prosecution's turn to cross-examine me
about the testimony I just gave. Monk's goal was obvious: to
try to discredit what I had just said and thereby minimize the
value of my expert testimony. He also hoped to make me
look foolish or uncertain of the facts in order to further un-
dermine my credibility in the judge's eyes.

Mr. Monk: I believe you said that Helen spoke openly about
being a bad mother. That she told you things that she
shouldn't have done.

Dr. Abramson: No. What I said was that when she discussed
her mothering, she would use the entire range of experiences; for example, that she doesn't cook enough. She
didn't attempt to portray herself as Super Mom. That's what
I meant to imply.

Mr. Monk: Did she say anything about herself that you
viewed as negative?

Dr. Abramson: No, she didn't.

Mr. Monk: Did she say anything about herself that would indicate that she was responsible for this child's conduct?
That is, the conduct that's been labeled as sexually acting
out?

Dr. Abramson: No. There is nothing in her behavior that
would indicate that.

Mr. Monk: Now, in your report, you said that Ms. Cross
openly discussed her sexual relationships.

Dr. Abramson: That is correct.

Mr. Monk: Did you ask direct questions about them?

Dr. Abramson: Yes, I did.

Mr. Monk: Doctor, do you know what an Oreo cookie is?

Dr. Abramson: Of course, but I can't see . . .

Ms. Douglas: Objection! What relevance can this possibly have?

At this point the judge called all three attorneys to the bench to discuss the matter off-the-record. An animated discussion ensued in hushed but heated tones. Unfortunately, I couldn't quite make out what was being said. Eventually, Monk resumed his questioning.

Mr. Monk: Again, do you know what an Oreo cookie is?

The Court: You may answer, Dr. Abramson.

Dr. Abramson: Yes, of course. I have young kids. They like Oreo cookies, particularly the ones with extra icing.

Mr. Monk: In what other contexts have you heard the term "Oreo cookie" used?

Dr. Abramson: I've heard it used as a racial slur to describe someone who is "black on the outside, but white on the inside."

Mr. Monk [agitated]: Dr. Abramson, how is it used with regard to *sex*?

Dr. Abramson: I don't think I've ever heard . . .

Mr. Monk [with evident disgust]: Isn't "Oreo cookie" another term for a *ménage à trois*?

Dr. Abramson: If so, I've never heard it!

The Court: Mr. Monk, if you wish to ask about sexual matters, please use plain English. It's easier for everyone involved.

Mr. Monk: Fine. Dr. Abramson, did you ask Ms. Cross
whether or not she's had relationships with women?

Dr. Abramson: Yes, I did.

Mr. Monk: And what was her response?

Dr. Abramson: She told me she had had a *ménage à trois*
and briefly attempted a relationship with a woman.

Mr. Monk: Did you ask her where her daughter was when
this was going on?

Dr. Abramson: No, I didn't.

Mr. Monk: Did you ask her whether that *ménage à trois* was
with two men or a man and a woman or what?

Ms. Douglas: Objection, relevancy.

The Court: Mr. Monk?

Mr. Monk: Your Honor, the focus of the case is both incest
and sexual play. The young girl, the minor, was in her
mother's custody. I think it is very relevant to determine the
nature of the mother's sexual conduct.

Monk's strategy was rather surprising—particularly in the
1990s. He was clearly attempting to malign Helen's integrity
by questioning her sexual history. Presumably, he wanted to
portray Helen as "immoral." One implication he might have
been trying to draw is that Helen is oversexed, hence more
likely to commit incest. However, this strategy is in direct op-
position to the scientific literature, which demonstrates that
pedophilia is a highly distinct predilection that is rarely present in heterosexual women, regardless of their sexual activ-

ity level. He also might have hoped that Judge Shriver would disapprove of Helen's wild—and some might say, irresponsible—sexual past. If the judge believed that Helen lacked morals, he might think she was less fit as a mother.

Moreover, as every good lawyer knows, it isn't necessary to change a judge's conscious thought patterns to affect a positive result. All that is needed is to tap into unconscious biases and to let hidden psychodynamic processes do the rest. Should Helen's past sexual exploits matter in this trial? The answer seemed obvious. But would they matter? The answer to this question was not nearly so clear.

Of course, the ultimate arbiter of this debate over the relevancy of Helen's sexual history to the present case was Judge Shriver, who ruled, in essence, that Helen's sexual behavior was not on trial. The question was not whether the judge or society approved of her sexual experimentation, but whether she had harmed her daughter.

Ms. Douglas: Your Honor, I would agree with counsel if he restricts his questions to sex with children. There is no indication that this incident has anything to do with children.

Mr. Monk: We are determining the sexual environment in which this child lived, Your Honor. I think the sexual conduct of the mother is important.

The Court: You may ask if the child was present during the sexual conduct. And you may inquire as to whether the sexual conduct involved children. But if it didn't involve children, or the child wasn't present, then it would be irrelevant to the case. The objection is sustained.

Mr. Monk: Would you describe Helen Cross as a promiscuous woman?

Ms. Douglas: Objection, relevancy.

The Court: Sustained.

Although Monk had hit a dead end, he did not give up the strategy of trying to damn Helen with her past sexual exploits. His persistence raised a red flag for me. Why, I asked myself, would he persist in this line of questioning? The judge had already given his opinion about the relevancy of Helen's sex life. I begin to wonder whether Monk had a sexual bombshell he planned to drop or whether he was just testing the waters. What, if anything, had he dug up?

Mr. Monk: Did you read in your reports a description of Katherine simulating a *ménage à trois*?

Dr. Abramson: No, I didn't. I read that she had sexual play with other kids, which of course, is common.

Mr. Monk: Doctor, do you believe that some behavior is inappropriate for children of certain ages?

Dr. Abramson: Yes, certainly.

Mr. Monk: And how do you interpret Mr. Bickel's report of Katherine simulating a *ménage à trois*? Do you believe that was suitable conduct for a girl her age?

Dr. Abramson: What I read from that report was that there was a little girl playing sexual games with two other little girls. This is not uncommon.

Mr. Monk: I mean, a *ménage à trois*. Doctor! That is . . .

Dr. Abramson: What I read was that she wanted two kids to lay on either side of her. I hardly think this is equivalent to a *ménage à trois* in the adult sense of that term. I believe Mr. Bickel's choice of words was very poor.

Mr. Monk: Do you think that such conduct by a child is reflective of her environment?

Dr. Abramson: No, I do not. Many children play sexual games, regardless of their environment.

Again, Monk was attempting to imply that Katherine was sexually advanced—sufficiently advanced to have engaged in a *ménage à trois* with other children! The whole notion was absurd. A girl playing childhood sex games with two other children is no more a *ménage à trois* than two boys playing sex games is indicative of homosexuality. All children play "doctor" or some form of "I'll show you mine if you show me yours," but few grow up to be exhibitionists. Most authorities draw a distinction between sex games and overt sexual behavior. Monk did not.

Had my testimony been a bit more accommodating, Monk would have advanced the next step in his path of logic, arguing that Katherine's *ménage à trois* was a direct reflection of her mother's sexual behavior. By this line of questioning he was trying to establish that, even if Helen had not personally molested her daughter, the sexually permissive environment in which she was raising her daughter might have contributed to her alleged premature sexualization. This would suggest, at a minimum, that Helen was an unfit mother, and possibly, that she had failed to adequately protect her child.

Mr. Monk: You were supplied with the police report, is that correct?

Dr. Abramson: Yes, I was.

Mr. Monk: And did you read the police report?

Dr. Abramson: Yes, very carefully.

Mr. Monk: Doctor, in that report the police officer asked Katherine if anyone hurt her vagina. She said, "Yes, somebody." Then, when the officer asked her who hurts her she responded, "I forget. I don't remember. No one does. When my vagina hurts." Did that incident strike you as significant in and of itself?

Dr. Abramson: I concluded that Katherine was confused.

Mr. Monk: Were you aware of the many incidents in the report describing the child as publicly masturbating and engaging in sexual play?

Dr. Abramson: Yes.

Mr. Monk: Did you read in the report where teachers said that Katherine explained her conduct by saying, "I got it at home, I learned it from Mommy."

Dr. Abramson: Yes, I did . . .

Ms. Douglas: Objection, Your Honor. Counsel is stating facts not in evidence. If counsel is quoting a teacher, then it should be quoted exactly. I do not believe Katherine said, "I got it at home."

Mr. Monk: I can be more precise if the Court prefers.

The Court: Please do, Mr. Monk.

Mr. Monk: Very well. The police report says the following: "The policeman asks this teacher what first alerted her to Katherine's situation. This teacher said it was due to her doing sexual things a lot. She would raise her dress and masturbate. The teacher asked Katherine why she would do these things. Katherine says that her mom does it to her and that they do it at home. Katherine said that her mom taught her how to do it." Do you think this girl is a liar?

Dr. Abramson: No, I do not. This report also indicates at other places that—

Mr. Monk: Thank you, Dr. Abramson.

Did these incidents—the sexual acting out—make you suspicious that this child was suffering something—internally or externally—making her do inappropriate things?

Dr. Abramson: Not necessarily. I did, however, feel that I should do a very careful assessment of Katherine, including interviews with her teachers, her mother, and other relevant parties.

Mr. Monk: Are you aware of a description of something called aspirin, that upon further description, really does not appear to be an aspirin?

Dr. Abramson: I never interpreted it that way.

Mr. Monk: Excuse me?

Dr. Abramson: I interpreted the report differently.

Mr. Monk: Do you recall, in any of the reports, Katherine talking about her mother inserting an aspirin in her vagina?

Dr. Abramson: I read something to that effect.

Mr. Monk: Do you remember anything about the minor's description of this aspirin that would lift your eyebrows?

Dr. Abramson: The entire report, as I have indicated, made me feel that it was important to do a careful, thorough investigation of these comments.

Mr. Monk: What about the dildo?

Ms. Douglas: Objection. First . . .

The Court: Sustained.

Mr. Monk: Okay. Do you remember the aspirin that the child was talking about on June 20th, 1997?

Dr. Abramson: Yes, I do.

Mr. Monk: What do you remember about it?

Dr. Abramson: First, I do not believe that she meant to use the word "in." I did an experiment . . .

Mr. Monk: Excuse me. Your Honor, would the Court instruct the witness to answer yes or no?

The Court: To the best of your ability, Doctor, if it can be answered yes or no, please answer it that way.

Dr. Abramson: Okay. I felt in this particular case I could not answer it yes or no.

Mr. Monk: Let me repeat my question. What do you remember about the description of the aspirin?

Dr. Abramson: She showed how large it was, and the report differs in terms of the length. At one point it was six inches, another time it was shorter.

Mr. Monk: Did it strike you that this was, in fact, aspirin?

Dr. Abramson: No, it did not.

Mr. Monk: In your opinion, do children ordinarily lie about sexual molestation?

Dr. Abramson: No. But I do not believe that Katherine was describing sexual molestation.

Mr. Monk: Now, just looking at the incidents we have gone over, would you say that this child was evidencing inappropriate behavior?

Dr. Abramson: No. Not without a thorough investigation.

Mr. Monk: Doctor, do you believe in the concept of excessive masturbation for a five-year-old child?

Dr. Abramson: Yes, I do.

Mr. Monk: Do you believe that this child reached that limit?

Dr. Abramson: I'm not sure. I don't think sufficient evidence has been provided.

Mr. Monk: What about the teacher's report?

Dr. Abramson: That report indicates only that Katherine masturbates in inappropriate places. Obviously, even once is too much at school.

Mr. Monk: Isn't this excessive masturbation?

Dr. Abramson: The term "excessive" refers to frequency. I have no idea whether she's masturbating night and day. All I know is that she occasionally masturbated at school. Furthermore, I have no idea how the word masturbation is being used. Does it refer to brief genital touching or to sustained genital rubbing?

Mr. Monk: Does she repeat the same pattern of masturbation in her house?

Dr. Abramson: I do not know.

Mr. Monk: Did you ask Helen whether or not she ever observed the child masturbating in the house?

Dr. Abramson: No, I did not.

Mr. Monk: Did you feel it was an important question?

Dr. Abramson: It's a good question, but I did not ask it. Instead, I asked Helen to describe Katherine's "sexual acting out." She indicated that it was primarily sexual play with friends or touching herself at school.

Mr. Monk: Did you ask Helen whether or not she ever observed her child in sexual play?

Dr. Abramson: I did. When she was over at a friend's house she saw Katherine and a little boy engaging in sexual play.

Mr. Monk: Is there a pattern in this child that warrants a mother's attention?

Dr. Abramson: Yes. And I believe that Helen was very concerned about this behavior. She put Katherine in therapy.

Mr. Monk: When did the mother put the child in therapy?

Dr. Abramson: I believe several months before she contacted me. There is, I believe, a letter from her therapist in the official court record.

Dr. Jansson's letter had been provided to Judge Shriver but not admitted as evidence in the trial because Dr. Jansson was unavailable to testify. I, personally, was never given a copy of the letter, so I could not testify as to its contents.

Mr. Monk: Why did she put the child in therapy?

Dr. Abramson: The mother and the principal of the Discovery Zone, whom I have also interviewed, talked about the masturbation at school. They decided that it was something that was therapeutically relevant, so they put the child in therapy.

Mr. Monk: Was that a proper decision?

Dr. Abramson: Yes.

Mr. Monk: Why?

Dr. Abramson: Because, as I indicated, any masturbation in an inappropriate place warrants concern.

Mr. Monk: Do you think that her behavior indicates that Katherine Cross has an emotional problem?

Dr. Abramson: I don't know. She is certainly acting inappropriately, however.

Mr. Monk: You mean the masturbation?

Dr. Abramson: Yes.

Mr. Monk: Thank you. Nothing further.

Ms. Escobar: Your Honor, I have a few questions.

The Court: Okay.

Monk's ignorance regarding childhood sexual behavior was impressive in a pathetic sort of way. I began to wonder why he had not consulted with his own expert psychologist. Apparently, Monk believed that the appropriateness of a behavior could be determined on the basis of frequency alone. Thus, masturbating once a week was okay, but doing it every day suggested pathology. He also chose to interpret the Neosporin as a dildo despite the gynecological exam, which indicated that Katherine's hymen was intact.

It was then Katherine's attorney's chance to ask me some questions. Julia Escobar had been appointed by the Court to represent Katherine's interests in this case. Julia was a Mendocino native who had been practicing family law for over thirty years. She was quite competent and she knew the local courts, including Judge Shriver. Fortunately, she was convinced that Helen had not molested Katherine and therefore believed that her client's interests would best be served by returning full custody to her mother.

Ms. Escobar: Dr. Abramson, you mentioned in previous testimony that you had questioned Katherine with regard to her statement about an aspirin. What technique did you use to elicit information about that topic?

Dr. Abramson: I asked her to play a game, to see if she could identify certain objects. I started the "game" by showing her a bottle of Pepto-Bismol, which she correctly identified as "diarrhea medicine." Next, I showed her a series of other things, one of which was aspirin and another of which was a tampon. My objective was to obtain data relevant to two issues: First, did she know what aspirin was, and second, did she have a concept of the vagina as an orifice?

Ms. Escobar: Beyond the aspirin, tampons, and Pepto-Bismol, did you ask her about any other items?

Dr. Abramson: Yes. I showed her eye drops, toilet paper, Band-Aids, shaving cream, and—um—toothpaste. In each case, I tried to make a game of it, so that she would feel comfortable. Many of the items she could correctly identify, and others she couldn't. I did the same thing with sexual anatomy, to find out what Katherine knew about sexuality.

Ms. Escobar: And with regards to her knowledge about sexual anatomy, did you find her to be more or less informed than was normal or usual for her age group?

Dr. Abramson: I found her to be just about the norm.

Ms. Escobar: In your report you say you showed Katherine a photograph of a statue?

Dr. Abramson: Yes. I showed her a "folkloric" statue of a man with a large erection. She looked at it and said, "I know what that is—it's a man on a camel."

Ms. Escobar: Was showing her the photo of the statue an attempt to elicit whether she had a tremendous interest in sex or sexual subjects?

Dr. Abramson: My primary objective was to find out what she knew about sex. I discovered that Katherine had very limited knowledge, except for a strong interest in pregnancy, particularly the changes in a woman's body.

Ms. Escobar: Was there anything Katherine said that would indicate that she had been subjected to sexual play with adults?

Dr. Abramson: No. She seemed to be an average kid, with an average level of awareness and understanding of sexuality.

Ms. Escobar: Did it seem to you, from what you were able to gather from your evaluation with her, that she had contacts with explicit sexual verbalizations?

Dr. Abramson: No. She appeared to have very little knowledge of sexuality other than knowing anatomically correct terms for the genitals.

Ms. Escobar: Did it seem to you that she had witnessed adult sexual behavior?

Dr. Abramson: No.

Ms. Escobar: And can you give me your basis for that conclusion?

Dr. Abramson: When I showed her drawings of nude couples lying down and hugging, she had no idea what they were doing.

Ms. Escobar: Okay. Did she seem to . . .

Mr. Monk: I object, Your Honor. No foundation sufficiently established to allow him to express his opinion.

The Court: The Court feels that Dr. Abramson is eminently qualified as an expert in this area and will allow the question. Overruled.

Ms. Escobar: When you spoke with Katherine with regard to her sexual behavior—for example masturbating—was she reluctant to talk to you about that subject?

Dr. Abramson: No, she wasn't. I found Katherine to be open in discussing every subject.

Ms. Escobar: What did she tell you about her masturbating?

Dr. Abramson: She discussed her masturbation at school. She knew that she wasn't supposed to do it, but she felt other kids did it as well. When I indicated to her that school was not the place to masturbate—that masturbation was something people do in private—she thought for a few seconds then asked, "How about when I'm at school and in private?"—meaning when nobody was around. I just looked at her. She shrugged her shoulders, because she knew what my answer would be.

Thus, I found her to be forthcoming. She was clearly able to express things to me that she knew were wrong. Then when I asked her about her mother, which again was a similar kind of circumstance, she indicated that her mother never touched her sexually.

Ms. Escobar: Had you interviewed both mother and daughter together?

Dr. Abramson: Together and separately. Though, when together, it was merely rapport building.

Ms. Escobar: And in these interviews, how would you characterize their interaction?

Dr. Abramson: Warm and affectionate. They seemed very close and well-bonded.

Ms. Escobar: Did you observe any signs of attempts by Ms. Cross to control Katherine's statements or behavior?

Dr. Abramson: None whatsoever. And in my interviews, I found Katherine completely open. We talked about things that could get her in "trouble" again, as well as things that had been previously problematic. In general, I found her to be a very open, extroverted, and assertive kid, especially in the second interview.

In the first interview, she was more restrained. After she became comfortable with me—and concluded that I was no threat—she was very talkative and very independent. As I have indicated to the Court, I have interviewed a large number of children. And that's not always the case.

Ms. Escobar: Did you feel that Katherine had been instructed about what to say?

Dr. Abramson: No. At times she was uncomfortable and restrained and afraid to talk; at other times, she talked very openly.

Ms. Escobar: When she was uncomfortable, how did she react?

Dr. Abramson: Where topics related to sexuality were concerned, she would try to change the subject, or she'd look away, or she'd talk about horseback riding again.

Ms. Escobar: Did you talk to Katherine about her separation from her mother?

Dr. Abramson: Yes, I did.

Ms. Escobar: And was she uncomfortable talking about that?

Dr. Abramson: No, she wasn't. She was very adamant about how she hated it.

Ms. Escobar: But she was not reluctant to talk about it?

Dr. Abramson: No, she was not.

Ms. Escobar: Okay, You explored the concept of the vagina as an orifice.

Dr. Abramson: Yes, I did.

Ms. Escobar: How was that explored?

Dr. Abramson: I asked her where her mother inserted a tampon. She said the anus. And then I used drawings and she indicated that the vagina was a surface organ.

Ms. Escobar: Why did you ask these questions?

Dr. Abramson: In the records, there are contradictions. For example, the police conclude that a dildo was inserted in Katherine's vagina. Yet, the gynecological report indicates that the hymen is intact, and nothing's been inserted into the vagina. So, I wanted to resolve this discrepancy, and designed several simple experiments to examine this issue.

In particular, I wanted to differentiate Katherine's use of the words "in" and "on" and to determine whether she used them correctly. As my report indicated, Katherine used those words interchangeably. Thus, "in" can mean "on," and vice versa. So, when she spoke of something being put "in" her vagina, she might have meant that something was put "on" her vagina. When this word usage is combined with her intact hymen, it seemed highly plausible that she was telling the officer that something was put "on" her vagina—which, according to Helen, was medicine.

Ms. Escobar: According to her teachers, Katherine also exposed herself to other children. Did you discuss that behavior with her?

Dr. Abramson: Yes, I did.

Ms. Escobar: And what did that behavior consist of?

Dr. Abramson: She didn't deny it, but she insisted that other kids do it as well, but only she gets caught. She attempted to convey that it was part of sexual play.

Ms. Escobar: There was also a reference to her having other children touch her vaginal area? Did you explore that with her?

Dr. Abramson: Yes, I did.

Ms. Escobar: And what was her explanation?

Dr. Abramson: She said it felt good.

Ms. Escobar: Okay. When you discussed the allegations, did you ask about her mother putting medication on her vagina?

Dr. Abramson: Yes, I did.

Ms. Escobar: Did she say that felt good too?

Dr. Abramson: Yes.

Ms. Escobar: Is sexual play a learned behavior?

Dr. Abramson: No. As I have indicated to the Court, masturbation has been observed in infants under one year of age.

Ms. Escobar: Thank you. No further questions.

The Court: Before we continue, I have a few questions for Dr. Abramson.

Doctor, you used the term "psychotic" with regard to the known cases of mother-daughter incest. Could you define your meaning of the word "psychotic"?

Dr. Abramson: Yes. According to DSM IV, a psychotic state of mind—particularly as it relates to schizophrenic disorders—is characterized by delusions, prominent hallucinations, and disorganized speech and behavior.

The Court: If you could clarify for the Court, what is DSM IV?

Dr. Abramson: It is the fourth edition, or update, of the *Diagnostic and Statistical Manual of Mental Disorders*, which is an encyclopedic guide to mental illness.

The Court: Thank you. Doctor, would you feel that any mother who participated in incest with her daughter would necessarily be psychotic?

Dr. Abramson: No, not necessarily. But that's the reason why all known cultures have strong incest taboos: to regulate a maladaptive behavior.

The Court: Doctor, you have expressed an opinion that the removal of Katherine from her mother's home would be extremely traumatic, particularly in light of the fact that she's been removed previously.

Let's assume for a moment that Katherine has, in fact, been molested by her mother. Would it be more detrimental to extract her from the home again, or to leave her there to participate in court-ordered psychotherapy with her mother?

Dr. Abramson: If I may, I'd like initially to respond to the first part of your hypothetical. As we are all aware, there is a movement to separate "one-time" incestuous offenses from repeated, predatory incestuous offenses. The underlying logic is that the removal and incarceration of a parent is further trauma for the child. Thus, if the perpetrator is redeemable, and the therapeutic outlook favorable, it serves the *child's* best interest to treat the parent and keep the child in the home. This is especially true if the parent and child have an otherwise good relationship. The real question is: what is more traumatic to the child, because the State's primary interest is to protect the child. In some cases it might be best to conclude, okay, you did this, let's treat it, and leave the child in the home. And in this particular case, if it were true that Helen had sexually stimulated Katherine, I would, in fact, recommend therapy, in large part because of the high quality of their relationship. Remember, also, that Helen, on her own initiative, put Katherine in treatment, with the hope of clarifying and resolving Katherine's issues.

The Court: Is it your opinion that Katherine's best interests would be served by her staying in the mother's home?

Dr. Abramson: Yes, it is. I believe Helen is a very responsible mother.

The Court: Would that opinion change if, in fact, the mother had participated in molestation and yet continued to deny that participation?

Dr. Abramson: I think that her own treatment would require an acknowledgment if, in fact, she molested her daughter. It is impossible to treat something that is denied. The etiology cannot be explored, corrective measures cannot be implemented, and victim empathy cannot be established.

Following this brief exchange with Judge Shriver it was once again Megan's turn to reexamine me. Dr. Carrier, the prosecution's expert psychologist, was expected to testify later that day, or the next, and Megan intended to use my testimony as a preemptive strike. Dr. Carrier had administered a battery of tests to Katherine in their limited time together. Megan knew that Monk would try to use this fact to suggest that Dr. Carrier had somehow gained unique insight into Katherine's psyche. Both she and I knew better, however. Although the use of standardized psychological tests is often appropriate, they have rarely been rigorously validated for issues relevant to sexual molestation. As an alternative, I prefer extensive interviews. With creativity and patience, children can open up and discuss potentially painful subjects, and once a trusting relationship has been established, most children will talk freely.

The Court: Ms. Douglas?

Ms. Douglas: Dr. Abramson, if you wouldn't mind, I would just like to clarify a few points. In your discussions with Helen Cross, did she tell you whether or not Katherine had ever witnessed sexual acts?

Dr. Abramson: Yes, she did. She said Katherine hadn't ever witnessed a sex act.

Ms. Douglas: Doctor, in your involvement with this case did you consult other experts?

Dr. Abramson: Yes, I did.

Ms. Douglas: And without advising what those other experts told you, can you tell us what experts that you contacted?

Dr. Abramson: I con⁺ ⁻d a board-certified gynecologist to get a second opinion oⁱ the gynecological report.

Ms. Douglas: Doctor, have you reviewed Dr. Carrier's psychological report?

Dr. Abramson: Yes, I have.

Ms. Douglas: And are you familiar with the tests which he performed on Katherine Cross?

Dr. Abramson: Yes, I am.

Ms. Douglas: Have you ever performed any of those types of tests yourself?

Dr. Abramson: Yes, I have.

Ms. Douglas: About how many would you say you have performed?

Dr. Abramson: At least 3,000.

Mr. Monk: Objection, Your Honor. Vague and ambiguous. What tests are we talking about?

Dr. Abramson: I can list them. The Rorschach . . .

Mr. Monk: If I might . . .

The Court: The objection is overruled. You can do that in cross-examination, or Ms. Douglas may ask for more detail.

Ms. Douglas: Thank you, Your Honor. Doctor, what tests are you speaking of?

Dr. Abramson: There's quite a number of them. The Rorschach, the TAT, the CAT, Doll Play, draw-a-person, the Bender Gestalt, the WAIS, the WISK-R—I can keep going.

Ms. Douglas: Had you chosen to do so, would you have been able to perform those tests on Katherine?

Dr. Abramson: Certainly. I have had considerable experience with all of them.

Ms. Douglas: And did you choose to perform those tests?

Dr. Abramson: No, I did not.

Ms. Douglas: Why not?

Dr. Abramson: Because they are not specific to the issues under consideration in this case. Also, many of them have questionable validity and reliability—particularly with a five year old. Which means they don't measure what they purport to measure, and they can not consistently come up with the same score.

Ms. Douglas: But some therapists use them to save time. Is that correct?

Dr. Abramson: Correct.

Ms. Douglas: No further questions, Your Honor.

The Court: Mr. Monk, do you have any further questions for Dr. Abramson?

Mr. Monk: Yes, Your Honor.

Mr. Monk: Doctor, in the summary of your report dated August 11, you say that the child is on the extreme end of normal variation in childhood sexual play.

Dr. Abramson: Yes.

Mr. Monk: What put Katherine on the extreme end of this normal variation?

Dr. Abramson: The evidence indicates that this child is very curious about sexuality and has exhibited masturbation and sexual play in an inappropriate situation.

Mr. Monk: And what is the significance of the fact that she was sexually acting out repeatedly in inappropriate places?

Dr. Abramson: It warrants attention. For example, why is she playing sexual games at school? Is it to get attention? Or is it because she is comfortable with sexual play, and she needs to learn discretion? Or is it, as has been suggested in this case, because she has been sexually molested, and therefore oversexualized?

I believe that Helen Cross did exactly what she is supposed to do when confronted with such questions. She took responsible action by putting Katherine in psychotherapy.

Mr. Monk: Do you think that her inappropriate sexual behavior is symptomatic of a problem in the child?

Dr. Abramson: It may or may not be.

Mr. Monk: Is it, in your opinion, in Katherine's case?

Dr. Abramson: I have no idea. I have not been doing therapy with her.

Mr. Monk: You have no idea whether it is or isn't a problem for Katherine?

Dr. Abramson: It is certainly a problem for Katherine. Look at the consequences. Whether it is a symptom of something else is another issue. Her therapist is trying to understand why she exhibits this behavior in an inappropriate situation.

Mr. Monk: Were you trying to understand that?

Dr. Abramson: I was concerned more about whether incest or sexual molestation occurred.

Mr. Monk: Do you believe that sexual molestation occurred by anyone?

Dr. Abramson: I have no evidence to indicate that any sexual molestation occurred, although I can't rule out the possibility.

Mr. Monk: In your studies, Doctor, have you run across cases where children who initially admit to molestation or sexual abuse eventually retract their story?

Dr. Abramson: Yes, I have.

Mr. Monk: Why do they retract?

Dr. Abramson: There are many reasons. I have been in-volved in cases where children have denied molestation, only to admit it years later. I have been involved in cases where children have said, yes, it occurred, and retract it un-der a variety of different circumstances, such as a physical beating by the parent.

Mr. Monk: What are some of the other reasons that they re-tract it?

Dr. Abramson: Fear, ridicule in school, shame, embarrass-ment, concerns for their parents, intimidation by parents, and so on, are some of the reasons.

Mr. Monk: Have you ever worked on a case where the child was afraid of retaliation by the parent and thus retracted the initial allegation of child abuse or sexual abuse?

Dr. Abramson: Yes.

Mr. Monk: Has Katherine been told that she's going to be taken away from her mother?

Ms. Douglas: Objection, calls for speculation.

The Court: Can you answer that question, Doctor?

Dr. Abramson: She was aware of why she was taken away from her mother. She believes that she is now permanently back with her mother.

Mr. Monk: You said she is aware of why she was taken away from her mother?

Dr. Abramson: Yes.

Mr. Monk: And why does she think she was taken away from her mother?

Dr. Abramson: Because of her comments to a teacher.

Mr. Monk: Do you think that a child of Katherine's age is capable of making such statements, and exhibiting this kind of conduct, without having been exposed to it in some way?

Dr. Abramson: What kind of conduct and what kind of behavior are you referring to?

Mr. Monk: The masturbation.

Dr. Abramson: All children masturbate.

Mr. Monk: The excessive masturbation. You, yourself, say she is on the extreme end of normal.

Dr. Abramson: I didn't say it was excessive. There is a big difference between excessive and inappropriate.

Mr. Monk: But you yourself said she's at the extreme end of normal. Is there a difference between extreme and excessive?

Dr. Abramson: I said she was at the extreme end of normal *variation*, which is a statistical concept.

Mr. Monk: But her behavior is extreme?

Dr. Abramson: I used the word "extreme" in a purely statistical manner, to indicate that on a bell-shaped curve, her behavior fits on the extreme end of normal variation, but it's still within normal limits or variation.

Mr. Monk: So, in your opinion, is Katherine normal?

Dr. Abramson: Yes, she is.

Mr. Monk: I have nothing further, Your Honor.

Monk clearly wanted to depict Katherine's sexual play as "abnormal" or "excessive," when it was neither. There is substantial variation in the expression of most human behaviors, masturbation included. Some people do it a lot, some never do it. But when does "a lot" become "excessive"? This is a difficult question to answer when phrased in absolutes, although one study of sexual behavior among children provides an ad hoc definition of "excessive masturbation": masturbation is "excessive" when it is practiced ten to fifteen times a day.

Generally, psychologists prefer to think of behavioral frequencies in relative, or statistical, terms. Many behaviors and human traits are distributed according to what is known as the "normal distribution," which is simply the bell-shaped curve with which we are all familiar (see the figure below). Human I.Q.'s, for example, follow a normal distribution: the height of the curve at any point represents the proportion of people who have that particular I.Q. The highest point on the curve (at the middle of the "hump") occurs at

an I.Q. of 100, which is the mean (average) I.Q. of the entire population. The curve is symmetric, meaning that there are as many people with I.Q.'s that exceed 100 as there are people with I.Q.'s less than 100. And at the extreme far right end (the "tail") of the distribution are the geniuses, whose extremely high I.Q.'s distinguish them from the rest of us. At the other end (the left "tail") are the unfortunate individuals who are considered severely mentally retarded or developmentally disabled.

Most of us, however, fall somewhere toward the middle of the curve, perhaps a bit higher or a tad lower than the average, but in any case well within the "normal range." This is what psychologists mean by "normal variation." Every behavior or trait exhibits variability, and most variability is within normal limits. It is only out in the "tails" of the distribution that a behavior can potentially be characterized as "abnormal," but even then, the distinction implied by this labeling is largely arbitrary.

One of the reasons that psychologists and other social scientists find the normal distribution to be such a useful descriptive tool is that it provides a way to quantify "normal variation." As it turns out, if a behavior is normally distributed, then 97% of all people will fall toward the center of the curve, between the limits depicted in the figure (technically, these limits are two "standard deviations" away from the mean).

Even when a behavior is not normally distributed, the same concepts apply. There was no evidence that Katherine's behavior was "excessive" in any statistical sense. She was clearly very active in her sexual play, but not abnormally so—that is, she was clearly within the limits of normal variation.

The Court: It's getting rather late, but if Dr. Abramson is willing, perhaps we can wrap up his testimony today. Doctor?

Dr. Abramson: Yes, by all means.

The Court: Ms. Escobar, you may proceed with your re-cross.

Ms. Escobar: Thank you, Your Honor.

Doctor Abramson, when you interviewed Katherine, were you aware that there was a device involved in her alleged sexual molestation?

Dr. Abramson: Yes, I was aware of that.

Ms. Escobar: Were you able to ascertain what it was?

Dr. Abramson: No, I wasn't. In large part because I found the report contradictory. The gynecological evidence indicated there was never anything . . .

Mr. Monk: Objection, Your Honor. There is no foundation laid that this witness is capable of commenting on the results of the gynecological examination, nor is there any evidence indicated to this Court that he had the child examined by a gynecologist.

The Court: Overruled. You may answer the question, Doctor.

Dr. Abramson: From my perspective, there is confusion in the reports. The psychologist's report, the police report and the Child Protective Services report assert that something was inserted in Katherine's vagina. Yet the Court-appointed gynecologist indicated that nothing has ever been inserted in her vagina, because her hymen is intact.

To help clarify, I did two things, one of which was to give the findings of the report—without the "molestation" conclusions and referral information—to a board-certified obstetric-gynecologist from UCLA. The second thing was to do the experiment I mentioned previously, to see if Katherine had any concept of the vagina as an orifice.

Ms. Escobar: And she did not?

Dr. Abramson: She did not.

Ms. Escobar: Thank you. Nothing further.

The Court: May the Doctor be excused?

Ms. Douglas: Yes, Your Honor. However, as previously stated, he will be remaining in the courtroom with all counsels' permission.

The Court: That is understood. Mr. Monk?

Mr. Monk: Yes, Your Honor.

The Court: All right. You may step down, Doctor. Thank you.

Dr. Abramson, the Court feels that the stipulation between the attorneys to allow you to sit in on the remainder of the trial is certainly an appropriate one in light of the research that you do.

Dr. Abramson: Thank you, Your Honor.

Overall, I felt my testimony had gone quite well. My main intent was to clarify Katherine's comments and behaviors, and to emphasize how responsive Helen had been to her daughter's needs. In the process I was able to relate several problems I had noticed with some of the other reports and to introduce the findings from my little experiments with Katherine.

I also learned that Monk was not above dragging Helen and Katherine through the mud to win his case. The next day he would have a chance to counter my testimony with testimony from his own expert psychologist. I was looking forward to hearing what this expert had to say.

Several other witnesses were also scheduled to testify during Friday's proceedings, including one of Katherine's preschool teachers, Marcia Osborn from Child Protective Services, the gynecologist who had examined Katherine, and, somewhat surprisingly, Mary Lopes. Initially, Helen too had wanted to testify with the hope of "clearing her good name." Megan, however, was adamantly opposed to this suggestion and eventually persuaded Helen that she had little to gain and everything to lose by testifying in court. The prosecution could not call her as one of its witnesses due to protections again self-incrimination, but if Megan called her to the stand, Monk could cross-examine. Megan and I had little doubt that Monk would capitalize on any such opportunity to attack Helen with innuendo about her sexual past, hoping to paint her as a sexual libertine and an unfit mother. So, Helen sat on the sidelines while others argued over her future and the fate of her relationship with her daughter.

THE TRIAL: DAY TWO

The next day I awoke early, feeling refreshed after a good long sleep in a four-poster bed at the MacCallum House. I

was relieved to have finished my testimony and was looking
forward to observing the remainder of the trial, which I felt
sure we would win. I was especially eager to hear the testimony of the prosecution's expert psychologist, Dr. Carrier. I
had never heard of him, and neither had any of the colleagues I had contacted, either at home or at UC Berkeley.
Plus, I was intrigued by Monk's earlier intimation that there
was something more to Helen's sex life than she had di-
vulged thus far. I believed that she had been honest and
forthright with me. Even if Monk had obtained new and incriminating information regarding Helen's past sexual indiscretions, he would face a major challenge convincing Judge
Shriver to allow it as evidence.

> **The Court:** Ms. Douglas, would you call your first witness,
> please.
> **Ms. Douglas:** Thank you. Now, this is both Mr. Monk's and
> my witness. We both subpoenaed her.
> **The Court:** Mr. Monk, you agree that Ms. Douglas should call
> this witness?
> **Mr. Monk:** Yes, Your Honor, I do.
> **Ms. Douglas:** Very well.
> **The Court:** Ms. Douglas, you may proceed.

The first witness to take the stand was Lisa Ann DeVries,
a teacher at Katherine's school who had witnessed her sexual play. The prosecution and defense had jointly called her
to testify, as both sides believed that she could provide
needed background testimony. As far as I could tell, she had
no particular ax to grind, she was just an attentive young
teacher who was concerned about one of her students.

Ms. Douglas: Ms. DeVries, where are you employed?

Ms. DeVries: At the Mendocino Discovery Zone.

Ms. Douglas: In what capacity?

Ms. DeVries: I'm a preschool teacher.

Ms. Douglas: Do you know Katherine Cross?

Ms. DeVries: Yes, she was one of my students.

Ms. Douglas: Is she still your student?

Ms. DeVries: No.

Ms. Douglas: In May of last year did Katherine Cross's behavior draw your attention?

Ms. DeVries: Yes, it did.

Ms. Douglas: Can you tell us what that was?

Ms. DeVries: Yes. I was doing recess duty outside, and I observed Katie and a friend playing with each other. She was taking the boy's hand and pointing to the vaginal area.

Ms. Douglas: What did you do?

Ms. DeVries: I called them over, and I told them that these are private parts. And this should not be done at school. Katie said, "We do it at home, and my mommy puts medicine on me, and when I put my panties up, it feels really gooshy."

Ms. Douglas: Were there any further discussions with her?

Ms. DeVries: No. That was it. She just went off playing with her friend.

Ms. Douglas: Did you later discuss this incident with Katherine's mother, Helen Cross?

Ms. DeVries: Yes.

Ms. Douglas: And who was present during this discussion?

Ms. DeVries: The director of The Discovery Zone, Cecily Ogilvie-Struff, and my immediate supervisor, Barbara Mayes.

Ms. Douglas: What was the nature of the discussion with Ms. Cross?

Ms. DeVries: Basically I just told her what had happened outside on the playground.

Ms. Douglas: What was Helen Cross's response?

Ms. DeVries: She listened very well. Her response was about the medication—it was some sort of liquid, she said.

Ms. Douglas: No further questions, Your Honor.

The Court: Mr. Monk?

Mr. Monk: Thank you, Your Honor.

Ms. DeVries, regarding this May 1997 incident, did you report it to somebody?

Ms. DeVries: Yes. I reported it to my immediate supervisor.

Mr. Monk: Why?

Ms. DeVries: Because of her words.

Mr. Monk: Precisely what words are you referring to?

Ms. DeVries: "We do it at home, my mom puts medicine on me," and so forth.

Mr. Monk: Why did you feel it necessary to report it to your superior?

Ms. DeVries: Well, basically, because of those words. I thought they were sort of different. I have never heard a child say that.

Mr. Monk: Have you ever seen Katherine masturbate while in school?

Ms. DeVries: No.

Mr. Monk: Have you ever seen any other child masturbate at school?

Ms. DeVries: No.

Mr. Monk: No further questions, Your Honor.

The Court: Ms. Escobar?

Ms. Escobar: No questions, Your Honor.

The Court: Thank you very much, Ms. DeVries. You are free to go.

The prosecution's next witness was Marcia Osborn, one of the two social workers who visited Helen and Katherine and, ultimately, removed Katherine from her home and placed her in foster care. (The other CPS worker, Matt Bickel, had not been called to testify in the case.)

Mr. Monk: Ms. Osborn, what do you do for a living?

Ms. Osborn: I am the chief social worker with Child Protective Services, Mendocino County.

Mr. Monk: As a social worker for Mendocino County, were you ever aware that Katherine Cross, a minor, was an alleged victim of child abuse?

Ms. Osborn: Yes.

Mr. Monk: What were the allegations?

Ms. Osborn: The allegations were that the child had been exhibiting sexualized behavior at preschool.

Mr. Monk: What was the source of that information?

Ms. Osborn: The source was Barbara Mayes, who is a teacher at the child's school.

Mr. Monk: And what motivated your agency to open a case?

Ms. Osborn: The information given to me was that the child was exhibiting a lot of sexual behavior, such as masturbating at nap time and mutual masturbation with other children in the day care center.

Mr. Monk: Did Barbara Mayes suggest that this girl was a victim of sexual abuse?

Ms. Osborn: Yes, she did.

Mr. Monk: Did your agency open up a case?

Ms. Osborn: Yes.

Mr. Monk: And were you the worker on that case?

Ms. Osborn: Yes.

Mr. Monk: And what did you do as the worker on this case?

Ms. Osborn: First I made several attempts to call Barbara Mayes to clarify some of the information that was on the initial referral to our department.

Mr. Monk: After you got this information, what was your next step?

Ms. Osborn: My next step was to refer the case to a law enforcement agency for follow-up.

Mr. Monk: To which agency?

Ms. Osborn: I initially referred it to the Mendocino Police Department and to Sergeant Kelves of the Child Abuse Investigation Team there.

Mr. Monk: And when did you close this case?

Ms. Osborn: I closed it May 11 of 1997.

Mr. Monk: Why did you close it then?

Ms. Osborn: I referred it to the proper agency for follow-up investigation. Also, the mother, Helen Cross, said she was willing to put her daughter in therapy. Actually, she was already in therapy. I also told her she needed to give the therapy findings to the police.

Mr. Monk: Did your agency on or about June 20th, 1997, re-open a case of sexual molestation of Katherine Cross?

Ms. Osborn: On June 10th I received a phone call from Cecily Ogilvie-Struff, who is the principal of the day care center. And the information she gave me . . .

Ms. Douglas: Objection, hearsay.

The Court: Sustained.

Mr. Monk: So, based on the information that you received on or about June 19th from Ms. Ogilvie-Struff, you re-opened this case. Is that true?

Ms. Osborn: Yes, I did.

Mr. Monk: Did you ever interview this minor?

Ms. Osborn: Yes, I did. I interviewed her on June 20th, 1997.

Mr. Monk: Where?

Ms. Osborn: At the child's residence.

Mr. Monk: And who was present at the time?

Ms. Osborn: Besides myself, another social worker from CPS named Matt Bickel, and Officer Mark Popper of the Mendocino Police.

Mr. Monk: While at the house, did you interview the minor without the presence of the mother?

Ms. Osborn: Yes, I did. In the child's bedroom.

Mr. Monk: And as a result of that interview, did you remove the child from the mother's house and take her to the station?

Ms. Osborn: I gave the information to Officer Popper and he and Matt Bickel and I made a joint decision to remove the child from the home.

Actually, Popper was informed of the decision *after* it had been reached by the two social workers during a private conference. Moreover, it became clear later that Bickel was the driving force behind the removal, despite the fact that he had barely spoken to Helen and had participated in Katherine's interview only as an observer.

Mr. Monk: Why did you remove her from the mother's house?

Ms. Osborn: Because the child made allegations . . .

Ms. Douglas: Objection, hearsay.

The Court: Sustained. Mr. Monk?

Mr. Monk: Did you feel it was in the child's best interests to remove her from the mother's house?

Ms. Osborn: Yes, I did. According to Matt Bickel, Helen Cross . . .

Ms. Douglas: Objection.

The Court: Sustained.

Mr. Monk: No further questions, Your Honor.

Before calling his next witness, Monk made a singular request that took everybody—the judge, Megan, and myself included—by complete surprise. Monk insisted that I should be asked to leave the courtroom during his witness' testimony. When Judge Shriver told him, in no uncertain terms, that I was going to stay, Monk became highly agitated.

Those of us in the courtroom could hear him yelling, "But it's not fair to *my* witness . . ." Before he could finish, however, the judge interrupted him, insisting that any further discussion should be "on the record." I was then asked to step out of the courtroom while the issue was resolved. The following is from the official court transcript.

> **The Court:** The record should reflect that Dr. Abramson has been asked to excuse himself from the court. Mr. Monk, I believe you have a motion, sir?
>
> **Mr. Monk:** Yes, I do, Your Honor. Your Honor, Dr. Carrier, one of the primary expert witnesses we have in our case, has asked to be able to testify without the presence of Dr. Abramson. This is something that he feels very strongly about.
>
> I know that I initially agreed to the stipulation that allows Dr. Abramson to remain throughout these proceedings. I also understand that Dr. Abramson wanted to do this for his research. However, Your Honor, considering Dr. Carrier's feelings, I ask that the Court to respect his wish that he be allowed to testify without Dr. Abramson being in the court.
>
> **The Court:** Ms. Douglas?
>
> **Ms. Douglas:** Your Honor, I contacted Mr. Monk the day before this matter was called to trial. I explained to him that I was requesting to all counsel that Dr. Abramson be allowed to sit in on the entire proceedings. His report clearly indicates that he has done the evaluation, and performed these services without fee, solely with the idea of using this case in his further studies and research. He was taken out of order for exactly that reason. Mr. Monk's objection does not in any manner seem appropriate. I did not attempt to mislead

Mr. Monk about why he was here, and I indicated that he would be here during the entire testimony. There was never any request that Dr. Carrier be present during Dr. Abramson's testimony. I would not have objected to it if they had. They have certainly benefited by the fact that our expert had been on first, which is out of order, and is very unusual, and I am sure they have used that information in preparing for their questioning of Dr. Carrier. I think that to now say they don't want Dr. Abramson in here because Dr. Carrier is unhappy about it is improper, and I'd ask the Court to deny the motion.

The Court: Ms. Escobar?

Ms. Escobar: Your Honor, as I previously indicated, I am surprised that this should become an issue with regard to a professional testifying. If it were a child, or perhaps an inexperienced witness, certainly I would think that the Court would need to take that into consideration. But we're talking about a professional. This was a stipulation which apparently Mr. Monk did not make clear to Dr. Carrier. Frankly, I think that's Dr. Carrier's problem. And I don't see a basis to withdraw the stipulation at this point.

The Court: The Court is going to allow Dr. Abramson to stay. First, there is a binding stipulation which permits him to stay. Second, consistent with section 346 of the Welfare and Institutions Code, the minor's parent has requested that he stay. Third, that section also allows a Judge to permit such persons that he or she deems to have a legitimate interest in the particular case, and the Court certainly feels that Dr. Abramson would qualify under that section, because of his research objectives. So, the Court would allow him to stay, and you may ask Dr. Abramson to return.

Ms. Douglas: Thank you, Your Honor.

The Court: Okay. Are you ready, sir?

Mr. Monk: I am ready, Your Honor.

The Court: All right. After lunch you may call Dr. Carrier.

When I returned to the courtroom, Megan quickly and discretely informed me of the unusual interaction that had just transpired.

Now this was interesting! What was Dr. Carrier afraid of? Why would my presence in the courtroom upset him? I am hardly an imposing figure and my persona is really relatively benign. Perhaps he was afraid that I would hear something that he didn't want me to hear. It probably didn't have anything to do with his report. I had already read and criticized it. Either there was something fishy about his credentials, which would come up in the process of qualifying him as an expert, or he just didn't want to embarrass himself in front of a colleague. I suspected it was the former.

Playing this hunch, I stopped Megan before she went to lunch and asked her for a copy of Dr. Carrier's resume. I told her that I had a feeling he was hiding something. She gave it to me, and when I found what I was looking for, I got out my cellular phone, and went to work.

What I discovered, first, was that Dr. Carrier's Ph.D. was not from an accredited school. This is not that unusual, particularly in a state like California, which gives the psychology license if you can pass the tests, regardless of the school you attended. However, Dr. Carrier also listed himself as an adjunct professor at the University of California at San Francisco, one of the country's premier medical schools. This was quite an accomplishment for someone with no academic publications and a nonaccredited Ph.D.

Using my credentials as a professor at UCLA, I called the personnel office at UCSF. Sure enough—they had no record of Dr. Carrier! I then called the department in question. They had never heard of him either. Whatever else Dr. Carrier was, he was not an adjunct professor at UCSF!

I immediately drove to the Kyoto Sushi Bar, where Megan Douglas was having lunch and told her the news. She was thrilled. Dr. Carrier had misrepresented himself, and now we had proof! Sensing blood, Megan couldn't wait to get him on the stand for a *voir dire* examination.

We reconvened at the courtroom at 1 p.m. Megan bided her time while Monk conducted his initial questioning. We both listened attentively, hoping that he would dig the hole deeper.

Mr. Monk: Doctor Carrier, what is your profession?

Dr. Carrier: I am a clinical psychologist—a Ph.D.

Mr. Monk: What is a clinical psychologist?

Dr. Carrier: A clinical psychologist is a person who has completed a degree—a Ph.D.—in psychology or another subject that's accepted by the Board of Medical Quality Assurance, and has completed 3,000 hours of internship, and has been licensed to practice in the state in which they are working.

Mr. Monk: What do you have to do to get the license?

Dr. Carrier: The course work, the internship, a written exam, and an oral exam.

Mr. Monk: Thank you, Dr. Carrier. Dr. Carrier, have you ever examined a minor by the name of Katherine Cross?

Dr. Carrier: Yes, I did.

Mr. Monk: And why did you examine her?

Dr. Carrier: The examination was requested by Child Protective Services of Mendocino, California, for purposes of assessing a possible molestation. It was also to aid in a treatment and placement plan.

Mr. Monk: Thank you. I now contend that Dr. Carrier is an expert who may render his opinion regarding the issues he has just described.

Ms. Douglas: I object, Your Honor. There is no foundation for Dr. Carrier's expertise other than he is a licensed clinical psychologist. What about the areas of sexual molestation and incest? I believe what counsel is attempting to say is that anyone who is a clinical psychologist is automatically an expert in the field that is before the Court today.

The Court: Do you wish to take the doctor on *voir dire*?

Ms. Douglas: Yes, Your Honor.

This was the opportunity Megan was waiting for. In her *voir dire* examination she hoped to show that Dr. Carrier was not qualified to serve as an expert in matters of molestation and incest, or at the very least, to unnerve the witness and make Judge Shriver doubt his competence. Notice how she methodically—but diplomatically—attacks Dr. Carrier's educational background and academic qualifications. Note also Dr. Carrier's nervous reactions when she questions him about these subjects.

Ms. Douglas: Dr. Carrier, what is your educational background?

Dr. Carrier: I have a bachelor's and a master's degree in psychology, and a Ph.D. in clinical psychology.

Ms. Douglas: Where did you receive those degrees?

Dr. Carrier: The bachelor's from California State University, Northridge, the master's and Ph.D. are from Pacific Far West University.

Ms. Douglas: Doctor, can you explain to the Court what the American Psychological Association is?

Dr. Carrier: The American Psychological Association is the psychological equivalent of the American Medical Association. It is the largest association for guidance and control of the psychology profession.

Ms. Douglas: Does the association approve the clinical psychological programs at different universities?

Dr. Carrier: That's one function, yes.

Ms. Douglas: And is Pacific Far West University's clinical psychology program approved by the American Psychological Association?

Dr. Carrier: No.

Ms. Douglas: When did you get your Ph.D., Doctor?

Dr. Carrier: I received my doctorate in June of 1994.

Ms. Douglas: Thank you. Where are you employed, sir?

Dr. Carrier: I am employed in several different manners, mostly in Fort Bragg. I am on the faculty of UCSF Medical School, and I teach part-time and I practice part-time.

Ms. Douglas: UCSF is the University of California at San Francisco?

Dr. Carrier: Yes, ma'am.

Ms. Douglas: What is your position at UCSF?

Dr. Carrier: I am a clinical instructor.

Ms. Douglas: Are you a clinical instructor or are you a clinical associate?

Dr. Carrier: Well, I think it's changed. I started out as a clinical instructor. I think it is now a clinical associate.

Dr. Carrier's eyes began to dart around the room, purposely avoiding mine. Megan, in contrast, was calm. She knew that Dr. Carrier had invented this position and that his testimony was a fabrication.

Ms. Douglas: What is the significance of that distinction, Doctor?

Dr. Carrier: Those determinations are made on the basis of time teaching in a graduate program.

Ms. Douglas: And does it take more time teaching to be a clinical instructor or a clinical associate?

Dr. Carrier: To tell you the truth, I don't pay a whole lot of attention to either of those titles. I think associate, but I am not really sure. At the time that I went on the faculty there two years ago, what I—at that time, I had no teaching experience at a graduate level.

Ms. Douglas: So, you have two years teaching experience?

Dr. Carrier: Yes, two years.

Ms. Douglas: Other than the University of California at San Francisco, have you ever lectured at the university level?

Dr. Carrier: No.

Ms. Douglas: And in what subjects are you an instructor at UCSF?

Dr. Carrier was starting to sweat, and to swallow repeatedly, in a state of obvious anxiety.

Dr. Carrier: I, um, I instruct in a wide variety of subjects. It is a residency program in family medicine. I teach a wide variety of subjects. I lecture on psychological testing, I lecture on diagnostic work, I lecture on interviewing techniques, skills, I lecture on personality disorders, I lecture on depression, anxiety. But it's not like a traditional university class where you would lecture two hours a day on a particular topic.

Ms. Douglas: Do you lecture there on the subject of molestation of children?

Dr. Carrier: In the process of—there have been a number of lectures specifically on that topic. And I also coordinate those efforts through teaching about that through our out-patient clinic, teaching the signs and effects of molestation to the physicians in the out-patient clinics.

Ms. Douglas: Do you ever give any lectures in the area of incest?

Dr. Carrier: Yes, ma'am.

Ms. Douglas: Can you tell us how often you have lectured on that topic specifically?

Dr. Carrier: None of my lectures are set up on a two per year or three per year basis. It's—if you are looking for a number, how many have I given or how often do I give them?

Ms. Douglas: How many have you given on the subject of incest?

Dr. Carrier: Nine or ten.

Ms. Douglas: That's over the last two years. Is that correct?

Dr. Carrier: At the university level.

Ms. Douglas: Have you written any books or articles on molestation?

Dr. Carrier: No, ma'am.

Ms. Douglas: Have you written any books or articles on incest?

Dr. Carrier: No, ma'am.

Ms. Douglas: Have you been published in any capacity in the areas of molestation or incest?

Dr. Carrier: No, ma'am.

Ms. Douglas: Have you been published in the area—I'm searching for the right word here—

Dr. Carrier: Doesn't matter because I am not published.

Ms. Douglas: Thank you for volunteering that.

I have no further questions, Your Honor. However, I would object to the doctor testifying in today's proceedings as an expert. I don't believe he is qualified in the area of molestation or incest, in particular. I believe his education and experience is somewhat general and not specific enough to qualify him as an expert in this case.

With this line of questioning, Megan had succeeded in making the witness feel insecure about his credentials, by highlighting his lack of publications. While this is not necessarily sufficient to disqualify him, it did have the effect of making his expertise suspect. Moreover, Megan's aggressive approach, coupled with Dr. Carrier's lying under oath about his affiliation with UCSF, had completely discomfited him, so that he came across in a strange and confused manner.

The Court: Mr. Monk?

Mr. Monk: Thank you.

Doctor, were you required to study the dynamics of both molestation and incest in order to obtain your license?

Dr. Carrier: I wasn't required to learn about those areas, but I spent 1,500 hours working with children and those issues came up.

Mr. Monk: Where did you work?

Dr. Carrier: At an internship with Children's Mental Health of Mendocino County.

Mr. Monk: And did the issue of molestation and/or incest come up there?

Dr. Carrier: Constantly.

Mr. Monk: And how often were you dealing with that issue?

Dr. Carrier: Often. I worked as a consultant for this court, doing psychological evaluations via the Probation Department and Child Protective Services. Over the last two years, I have seen an average of four new cases per week.

Mr. Monk: Were you working as a clinical psychologist?

Dr. Carrier: Yes, sir.

Mr. Monk: What did you do as a clinical psychologist?

Dr. Carrier: Mostly evaluations. An evaluation consists of five different pieces, the first being a clinical interview and history. Next, there is testing, which is divided into four areas: intellectual functioning, scholastic achievement, neurological screening, and personality, and those are integrated then into the evaluation.

Mr. Monk: Is this what you did with Katherine Cross?

Dr. Carrier: With the exception of the scholastic achievement test, because of her age.

Mr. Monk: Thank you, Doctor.

I renew my motion to have this witness qualified as an expert in this field, Your Honor.

The Court: Ms. Escobar?

Ms. Escobar: I have no questions at this time, Your Honor.

The Court: Ms. Douglas?

Ms. Douglas: Same objection, Your Honor.

The Court: The objection is overruled.

Mr. Monk, you may inquire of the doctor as an expert.

Mr. Monk: Thank you, Your Honor.

Unfortunately, the judge was not aware that Dr. Carrier had misrepresented his credentials, and Megan could not raise the issue because it had not been substantiated. However, Megan had been successful in making Dr. Carrier nervous, which was an important victory. (It turns out that he had lectured to a group of medical students at UCSF on a single occasion. But, on his resume, that one lecture grew to a clinical professorship.)

Mr. Monk: Doctor, did you examine the mother, Helen Cross?

Dr. Carrier: No, sir.

Mr. Monk: But you did examine the child, Katherine Cross?

Dr. Carrier: Yes, sir.

Mr. Monk: And how long was your examination of Katherine Cross?

Dr. Carrier: I spent an hour and 45 minutes to two hours with her. Somewhere in that ballpark.

Mr. Monk: Doctor, when you examined the minor, what were you primarily looking for?

Dr. Carrier: I was trying to understand why she was saying one thing at one time and later something else. I was looking for any evidence of emotional disturbance that would give an indication that there had been something bothering her for some length of time. I was looking at the intellectual functioning, and I was looking at present emotional functioning.

Mr. Monk: Before you examined her, were you supplied with any information about her?

Dr. Carrier: Yes, I was. Reports from Child Protective Services and the police.

Mr. Monk: Before you examined her, did you think that she had been the victim of sexual molestation?

Dr. Carrier: It would have been premature to conclude that, but there were very strong indications that something was going on.

Mr. Monk: Based on what you read, without ever seeing the child, did you believe that this child was not normal in her sexual curiosity or activity?

Dr. Carrier: You have to first define what you are talking about as normal.

Mr. Monk: Based on the information that you were presented before you ever met this child, would say she was outside the normal range?

Dr. Carrier: Yes, sir.

Mr. Monk: When a psychologist concludes that a child is outside the normal range, does that have any significance to the psychologist who is about to examine the child?

Dr. Carrier: Well, yes, especially if the behavior is defined as a problem by someone.

Mr. Monk: In this case, was it defined as a problem?

Dr. Carrier: To my knowledge, yes, it was. It was defined as a problem by the school and it was defined as a problem by Child Protective Services.

Mr. Monk: Now, when you examined the child herself, what did you determine about her sexual preoccupations or sexual thoughts?

Dr. Carrier: At the time I saw her, as is documented in my report, she was denying that any "sexual acting out" had ever occurred. In fact, whenever the topics of sex or her mother came up, she would become agitated, fidgety, try to change the subject, or try to push the testing materials away. That led me to believe that there is a problem in those areas.

Mr. Monk: Are you able to be more specific as to what that problem is?

Dr. Carrier: I believe that Katherine is trying to pretend that the sexual acting out never happened. She's trying to repress it. And there must be a reason she's doing that.

Mr. Monk: Such as?

Dr. Carrier: In the initial phase of an investigation, young children speak truthfully because they are unaware of the consequences of their statements. Once the statements are made, however, traumatic events can occur—including removal from the home. At that point, the child is aware that the statements resulted in traumatic consequences.

Eventually, the child starts thinking, "If I deny that I said those things, and deny that those things happened, they will send me back home and everything will be fine." That's a very common phenomenon in molestation cases.

Mr. Monk: Do you think Katherine is denying sexual activity because she's afraid she's going to be removed from her mother's house?

Dr. Carrier: Yes.

Mr. Monk: Do you think she is denying everything that she has admitted to in the past? That is, did you ask her whether or not her mother put something in her vagina?

Dr. Carrier: Yes, I did.

Mr. Monk: And what did the child say?

Dr. Carrier: She said no.

Mr. Monk: What questions did you ask about her sexual activity?

Dr. Carrier: I got denials across the board about whether she had been masturbating at school, masturbating at home, or trying to insert things into her vagina. She was also real nervous—fidgeting, changing the subject, and pushing things around.

It is important to note that Dr. Carrier spent a total of only two hours with Katherine, which included all of his tests (which he did not personally administer) and the "interview." The pivotal issue is whether Katherine felt comfortable enough with him during this brief interaction to answer any of his questions directly or honestly. As I mentioned in my testimony, Katherine was initially reticent to discuss sexuality with me, reacting just as Dr. Carrier describes: by fidgeting, changing the subject, and so forth. But, once we had established a comfortable rapport and she had come to trust me, she freely admitted engaging in masturbation and other forms of sexual play.

Mr. Monk: Did you test the child for her intelligence?

Dr. Carrier: Yes, I did.

Mr. Monk: How did she score?

Dr. Carrier: Very high. On the Wexchler preschool and primary scale of intelligence, she had a verbal I.Q. of 131, performance I.Q. of 120, and a full-scale I.Q. of 129.

Mr. Monk: Do you believe that this intelligence plays a role in understanding the child?

Dr. Carrier: I am not sure of your question?

Mr. Monk: Do you think that the child is denying the truth?

Dr. Carrier: She is denying what's been stated in the reports.

Mr. Monk: Doctor, based on the reports, do you believe that this girl was sexually acting out?

Dr. Carrier: Yes, I do. Usually the initial statements that a child makes in the process of an investigation like this are the truth, and then after consequences are placed on those statements, invariably those statements change.

Mr. Monk: Doctor, in your report on page 4, the first paragraph ends in the following sentence, "There is no doubt in my mind that she has been subjected to sexual play, explicit sexual verbalizations and has probably witnessed sexual activity." Is that correct?

Dr. Carrier: Yes.

Mr. Monk: Do you believe that there has been damage or a problem created for this child because of her exposure to the sexual activity?

Ms. Douglas: Objection, assumes facts not in evidence.

Mr. Monk: Your Honor, the doctor has said that there is no doubt in his mind that this child has been subjected to sexual play, sexual verbalization, and has probably witnessed sexual activity.

The Court: The objection is overruled. You may cross-examine him as to the basis for his opinion.

Mr. Monk: Do you believe that at the time you examined the child, she had been damaged because of this exposure?

Dr. Carrier: Yes. I believe she has a problem. I believe that damage has been done.

Mr. Monk: What kind of damage?

Dr. Carrier: It fits in with the concept of her world falling apart and her security being threatened. According to the information that I was given, the sexual acting out had occurred over a fairly extensive period of time. Suddenly, people started saying that it was wrong. This creates instability. The child feels castigated.

Mr. Monk: Consider the nature of the child's problem and the fact that it has been going on for years, do you think that the child would have masturbated and conducted herself sexually in the home . . .

Ms. Douglas: Objection, stating facts not in evidence. There's no evidence that it's been going on for years.

Mr. Monk: Your Honor, I believe that the reports will indicate that it was in Thanksgiving of 1995 that Helen Cross first became aware of an incident involving sexual abuse. And I believe that throughout 1996 and 1997, the reports will indicate that the child was exhibiting the sexual conduct.

The Court: I will allow the question. Again, you may cross-examine on the issue.

Dr. Carrier: Okay. It would be almost inconceivable to me that the sexual acting out was not happening at home—given the extent to which it occurred at school.

Mr. Monk: Do you think the mother should have been aware of this conduct?

Dr. Carrier: Yes.

Mr. Monk: Doctor, do you believe that it would be in the best interest of the minor to be taken out of her mother's environment?

Dr. Carrier: That's a big question. Because of the ramifications there are some other things that need to be established before that question is answered directly.

Mr. Monk: Such as?

Dr. Carrier: Does she need to be taken out of the home in order to get treatment? I think that's the crux of the question. And from my experience, there have been major resistances by Ms. Cross to this process. She didn't want her child evaluated by me. And I believe that she coached her child not to talk. That raises a major issue, in my mind, about whether or not in-home placement is appropriate.

Mr. Monk: What troubles you most about this case?

Dr. Carrier: Inserting objects into her vagina. That behavior is learned. None of us are born with that knowledge. And because it went on for a period of time, without Helen Cross doing something about it, leads me to the conclusion that she was condoning that behavior and was saying that that behavior was okay.

Despite Dr. Carrier's testimony, there never was any factual evidence that anything had been inserted into Katherine's vagina. (Indeed, the intact hymen would argue otherwise.) Even if she had inserted objects into her vagina, the notion that this is necessarily a learned behavior is absurd. Many young girls first discover their vaginal canal as a result of sexual self-exploration.

> **Mr. Monk:** As a psychologist, does that lead you to have doubts about Ms. Cross's ability to parent this child?
>
> **Dr. Carrier:** Yes, it does.
>
> **Mr. Monk:** Do you believe, in consideration of Katherine's reported sexual activity and based on your examination, that this child has been the victim of neglect?
>
> **Dr. Carrier:** Can you define what you mean by neglect?
>
> **Mr. Monk:** Do you believe that Katherine's emotional growth has been endangered by her mother?
>
> **Dr. Carrier:** Her healthy emotional growth, yes.
>
> **Mr. Monk:** Do you think we should intervene and make this child a dependent of the court?
>
> **Dr. Carrier:** Yes, I do.
>
> **Mr. Monk:** Based on what you know, do you believe that Katherine will experience serious emotional problems if she isn't properly treated?
>
> **Dr. Carrier:** Yes, I do.
>
> **Mr. Monk:** Do you doubt Ms. Cross can be responsible for the proper treatment and counseling of this child's problems?
>
> **Dr. Carrier:** Yes, I do. I do not think she would be willing to do it.

Dr. Carrier made this statement despite the fact that Helen had *already* placed Katherine in therapy, and in apparent ignorance of the opinion of Katherine's therapist, Dr. Janssen, who had concluded that mother-daughter incest had not occurred. Dr. Carrier was making large leaps in his testimony, with the apparent intent being to get the judge to remove Katherine from Helen's custody. This, of course, was Child Protective Services' objective, and the prosecutor's as well.

Mr. Monk: Considering the problem and considering the child, how critical is counseling in the next several years?

Dr. Carrier: In my experience, if it is not treated effectively within the next several years, it will plague her as a teenager or adult. Major problems will start interfering with normal activities of life, school work, and relationships.

Mr. Monk: Is it in the best interest of this minor that she be made a dependent of this Court?

Dr. Carrier: As I said before, yes, I believe it is.

Mr. Monk: Thank you. Nothing further, Your Honor.

The Court: Ms. Douglas?

From his testimony it was apparent that Dr. Carrier was either an unscrupulous psychologist or a very misinformed one. As it turned out, he was a little of both—blatantly biased and unwittingly deceived. He was biased by the (dis)information he had received from Matt Bickel, which led him to form preconceived conclusions about Helen, her daughter, and the relationship between them. Despite interviewing Katherine, he never actually *listened* to her. If he had, he might not have been so easily swayed by Bickel's duplicity.

> **Ms. Douglas:** Doctor, the time you spent with the Katherine was about an hour and forty five minutes to two hours.
>
> **Dr. Carrier:** Yes, ma'am.
>
> **Ms. Douglas:** Did that include the time it took to take the tests?
>
> **Dr. Carrier:** Yes, it did.
>
> **Ms. Douglas:** And that was approximately half a dozen tests?
>
> **Dr. Carrier:** Yes, ma'am.
>
> **Ms. Douglas:** How much of that hour and 45 minutes was for testing, and how much for the interview?
>
> **Dr. Carrier:** The interview was 20 to 25 minutes. And with children of that age, you got to get the child settled down, and then the interview is interspersed throughout the testing.
>
> **Ms. Douglas:** So, the interview . . .
>
> **Dr. Carrier:** I would say total time, total time spent on the interview, as opposed to testing questions, was 20, 25 minutes.
>
> **Ms. Douglas:** Thank you, Doctor. Who had you spoken to from Child Protective Services to get the background information?
>
> **Dr. Carrier:** Mr. Matt Bickel.
>
> **Ms. Douglas:** And how many times did you speak with Mr. Bickel?
>
> **Dr. Carrier:** It was several times. Three, at least.

Ms. Douglas: Other than speaking with Mr. Bickel, did you speak to anyone else from Child Protective Services?

Dr. Carrier: No.

Ms. Douglas: When you interviewed Katherine Cross, were you looking to the question of whether the child was a victim of sexual molestation?

Dr. Carrier: I was looking for any evidence of emotional disturbance. In a psychological evaluation interview, you cannot prove or disprove that molestation has occurred, unless that person says so. These instruments do not prove that a molestation took place. Physical exam does that.

Ms. Douglas: Can you gain insight into the question of whether molestation took place?

Dr. Carrier: Yes, ma'am.

Ms. Douglas: So, during this interview you were . . .

Dr. Carrier: I was looking for any indications of an emotional disturbance that had been interfering with normal development. And that would be evidence that a molestation had occurred.

Ms. Douglas: Thank you, Doctor.

If a parent is told that a child, age five, is sexually acting out, what is the proper course of action for that parent to take?

Dr. Carrier: The proper course of action, in my opinion, is to determine why those actions are occurring, and then take steps to correct that. If you are talking about behavior, you are talking about psychological counseling.

Ms. Douglas: In Katherine's situation, would the appropriate professional person be a therapist, such as a psychologist?

Dr. Carrier: Yes, it would.

Ms. Douglas: Are you aware that Katherine was seeing a therapist, at her mother's initiation?

Dr. Carrier: No. I don't believe that is true.

Ms. Douglas: Doctor, in reading your report, am I correct in assuming that you found it significant that Katherine denied the sexual acting out?

Dr. Carrier: Yes, I did.

Ms. Douglas: And you found it significant that she became agitated and nervous by your questioning.

Dr. Carrier: Yes, ma'am.

Ms. Douglas: I believe you also stated that Katherine's denial indicated that she was receiving pressure from someone?

Dr. Carrier: That is true.

Ms. Douglas: And you spent approximately 20 to 25 minutes interviewing her?

Dr. Carrier: Yes, ma'am.

Ms. Douglas: Is it likely, Doctor, that any child would want to openly discuss something as sensitive as sexual acting out with a total stranger after only having met that person within the last 20 minutes?

Dr. Carrier: Can I explain?

Ms. Douglas: Let me ask the next question. Would it be difficult for a child to talk when she had previously been removed from her home and her mother?

Dr. Carrier: Yes.

Ms. Douglas: Might she be nervous explaining her actions at school?

Dr. Carrier: No, ma'am. A five-year-old child is not capable of abstract thought.

Ms. Douglas: Can a five-year-old say things that aren't true?

Dr. Carrier: Yes.

Ms. Douglas: Is it possible for a five-year-old child to make up a story when she is confronted in a negative manner?

Mr. Monk: Objection, Your Honor. Vague.

The Court: Do you feel that you can answer the question?

Dr. Carrier: I'm not sure what she's asking.

The Court: Sustained.

Dr. Carrier had been called as an expert witness, someone, based upon his or her credentials, background, and training, who can facilitate the decision making of a judge or jury. While we often think of an expert witness as a professor, the designation of "expert" can be applied to anyone who is highly skilled in an area relevant to the case at hand. Thus, in a trial involving the business practices of a taxi company, a taxi driver could potentially qualify as an "expert witness." Conversely, despite his doctoral degree, the expertise of Dr. Carrier was certainly suspect.

Where the testimony of an expert witness is concerned, rigorous standards of scientific evidence still prevail. If an expert witness proclaims scientific authority, he or she must be speaking of a science that is falsifiable, well-established in peer-reviewed professional journals, explanatory, and consistent with the methods and theories of science. This is true regardless of whether the expert is a physicist, psychologist, physician, or social worker.

Psychology and psychiatry, unfortunately, are notorious for their disregard of science in the courtroom. The use of psychological tests is especially problematic. Most psychological tests have such poor records of validity and reliability that they are virtually useless in a forensic setting. They are just as likely to get it wrong, as to get it right. (A "valid" test is one that actually measures what it purports to measure; a "reliable" test is one that generates reproducible results.)

Often the psychological tests introduced in expert testimony are tangential to the specific issues under consideration. For example, the I.Q. test administered by Dr. Carrier had little relevance to the critical question of whether Katherine had been sexually abused by her mother. The same could be said of tests of anxiety, depression, or self-esteem. Anxious, depressed and low-self-esteem kids are not necessarily the offspring of sexually molesting mothers. In fact, we would argue that it was rarely so, based upon the very low prevalence of mother-daughter incest and the many other causes of depression, anxiety and low self-esteem.

Moreover, given the problems with the tests themselves, it seems unconscionable that an expert would use psychological tests with limited reliability and validity—particularly ones that bear no causal relationship with the issues under consideration. Worse yet, it seems especially galling that an expert would make a diagnosis, without reference to relevant base rates, using psychological tests that have great difficulty "separating the wheat from the chaff."

Dr. Carrier concluded that Katherine was sexually molested by her mother because she was reticent to speak to him. She was, in essence, "defensive" around him. Presume, for purposes of discussion, that Dr. Carrier gave Katherine a psychological test, and she was characterized as "very defensive." What information does this test result actually provide? Without a baseline to compare it with, an isolated test result provides no indication of the impact that the specific event (alleged sexual molestation) had on Katherine's present-day, or future, functioning. Moreover, acting "defensive" is not a specific indicator of mother-daughter incest. Children can be defensive for many reasons. Thus, the test has no discriminant validity. Furthermore, if the test itself is unreliable, Katherine might appear "very defensive" today, but "very open" tomorrow. Such are the foibles of psychological tests.

If psychological tests are problematic, what are the alternatives? Because the role of the expert witness is inherently subjective (particularly where psychological issues are concerned), experience and knowledge of specific, relevant content areas are critical. Thus, when looking for an expert on incest it is preferable to use someone who has worked with incest victims (or perpetrators), who understands their psychological motives and defenses, and presents a tenable, logical, and scientific (if just theoretical) rationale for his or her beliefs. The basis for expert testimony does not presuppose that the expert's beliefs are necessarily true, only that his or her opinions are well founded and solidly based on the available evidence and on scientific knowledge. Ultimately, it is up to the judge or jury to weight the expert's opinions according to how compelling they find them.

Ms. Douglas: Doctor, in your report, you describe Katherine as a disturbed child. Could you please define for us the word "disturbed"?

Dr. Carrier: A disturbed child is a child who has a preoccupation with a behavior or situation.

Ms. Douglas: What is your basis for classifying Katherine as a disturbed child?

Dr. Carrier: The change in anxiety level.

Ms. Douglas: When to when, Doctor?

Dr. Carrier: The change in anxiety level when I tested her.

Ms. Douglas: Is there anything else?

Dr. Carrier: She thinks her world is falling apart.

Ms. Douglas: You are classifying Katherine as a disturbed child because she was nervous during the testing and because of the anxiety she was experiencing as a result of being taken out of her home?

Dr. Carrier: And the preoccupation with sexual behavior. That is a very strong indicator that there is some disturbance going on.

Ms. Douglas: How many incidents would it take for you to conclude that there was excessive sexual acting out?

Dr. Carrier: In Katherine's case, there are numerous incidents that occur over an extended period of time.

Ms. Douglas: Could you please be more specific, Doctor? What period of time?

Dr. Carrier: I recall from the school reports, there were numerous instances of removing her pants and masturbating and trying to shove objects into her vagina.

Ms. Douglas: How numerous?

Dr. Carrier: It was going on for three or four months.

Ms. Douglas: Doctor, in your report, you state that Katherine has been exposed to explicit sexual verbalizations. Can you elaborate on that?

Dr. Carrier: Yes. The situation where she told one girl, "You be a boy," and told the other girl, "You be a boy, and I'll be in the middle," is an ordeal that I've never seen in textbooks or taught in any school.

Ms. Douglas: And you recall reading a report indicating that all of those statements were made by Katherine Cross?

Dr. Carrier: Yes, ma'am. Besides that, five-year-olds do not say such things unless they have heard them elsewhere.

Ms. Douglas: Can a five-year-old masturbate without seeing it elsewhere?

Dr. Carrier: Yes.

Ms. Douglas: Your conclusions, Doctor, are based, if I'm correct, at least in part on statements that were made to you and information you received from others. Is that correct?

Dr. Carrier: That's correct.

Ms. Douglas: Who was the main source of that information?

Dr. Carrier: Mr. Bickel provided me with the reports, and I talked to him several times.

Ms. Douglas: Do you remember what Mr. Bickel told you?

Dr. Carrier: He made a synopsis of the information. He said they had a strong case against Helen Cross.

Ms. Douglas: Doctor, I think I counted three times where you referred to Katherine inserting objects into her vagina. What is the basis is for your making those statements?

Dr. Carrier: Well, Mr. Bickel. But inserting things in her vagina was mentioned in the school reports too, wasn't it?

Ms. Douglas: Did you assume that the reports you were given were true?

Dr. Carrier: Not necessarily a hundred percent correct, but there was no motivation for the school to lie.

In actuality, the school reports never mentioned anything about Katherine inserting anything in her vagina. The reports, therefore, hadn't lied. Indeed, as Dr. Carrier asserted, they had "no motivation to lie." The same could not be said about Bickel, who was a source of misinformation throughout the proceedings. His motives, however, would only become clear much later in the course of the trial.

Ms. Douglas: When Mr. Monk inquired whether Katherine should be removed from her home, your response, as I recall, was a couple of issues needed to be addressed before that determination could be made.

Dr. Carrier: Correct.

Ms. Douglas: First, you stated, she is going need proper treatment. Could you please tell us again what the second issue was?

Dr. Carrier: Okay. The other issue centers around eliminating a long-standing behavior.

Ms. Douglas: How long?

Dr. Carrier: Two years.

Ms. Douglas: You were told that it was two years?

Dr. Carrier: Yes, Matt Bickel said it was two years. And he said the mother knew about it. A prudent person would have done something about it prior to notification by the school. This mother resisted the authorities. She wasn't interested in finding out what was going on, but instead, had her own resistances.

Ms. Douglas: Could you please tell us what you are saying? What are these resistances you keep mentioning?

Dr. Carrier: Refusing to have *my* psychological evaluation done.

Ms. Douglas: Excuse me, Doctor. So when you said Helen resisted getting Katherine proper treatment, you meant she resisted being interviewed?

Dr. Carrier: Well, yes, I . . .

Ms. Douglas: And what is the basis for your statement that Ms. Cross resisted your evaluation?

Dr. Carrier: She didn't refuse directly to me. CPS told me that she initially refused to have the evaluation.

Ms. Douglas: Who told you that, Doctor?

Dr. Carrier: Matt Bickel.

Ms. Douglas: Thank you. Doctor, have you seen Katherine Cross since July?

Dr. Carrier: No, I haven't.

Ms. Douglas: Where have you gotten information about her in the last four months?

Dr. Carrier: From Matt Bickel.

Ms. Douglas: And what resistances did he mention had occurred in the last four months?

Dr. Carrier: Refusal to give CPS any kind of access to whoever the therapist is involved in the case. And I believe—I may be off base with this, but I believe there was also a request that Ms. Cross undergo a psychological evaluation.

Ms. Douglas: Is that one of the reasons you concluded that Helen Cross was resistant?

Dr. Carrier: Yeah.

Ms. Douglas: I have no further questions.

This case had taken some very unusual turns. It featured an expert (Carrier) who relied upon second-hand information, as well as a social worker from Child Protective Services (Bickel) who obviously had no regard for the truth. Little did I know it would only get stranger.

The Court: The witness is yours, Ms. Escobar.

Ms. Escobar: Thank you, Your Honor.

Ms. Escobar: Dr. Carrier, when you interviewed Katherine, how much time did you take getting to know her?

Dr. Carrier: The rapport-building goes on through the entire process.

Ms. Escobar: But, excluding the time spent taking tests, how much time did you spend talking to her?

Dr. Carrier: About twenty minutes.

Ms. Escobar: It indicates in your report that at one point you confronted Katherine with regard to her denial of "sexual-acting-out" behavior. How did you confront her?

Dr. Carrier: I asked her whether or not she had been masturbating in school. I asked her whether or not she had been involved in a situation that I talked about before—the girl on each side and her in the middle. I asked if she had ever attempted to touch any other child's private parts. That's what I mean by confronted.

Ms. Escobar: You questioned her? That's what you mean by confront?

Dr. Carrier: Yeah.

Ms. Escobar: She denied that she had done these things. Is that correct?

Dr. Carrier: Yeah.

Ms. Escobar: Did you indicate to her that you did not believe what she was saying?

Dr. Carrier: Now, I don't—I mean I never—I don't ever indicate to a child that I don't believe them.

Ms. Escobar: But you didn't believe her. Is that correct?

Dr. Carrier: That's correct.

Ms. Escobar: Thank you. Nothing further.

The Court: Mr. Monk, redirect examination?

Mr. Monk: Yes, Your Honor. Why didn't you believe the child, Doctor?

Dr. Carrier: Because in my experience in working with molested children, which is fairly extensive, the truth comes out in the first statements they make. It's a common phenomenon that after a child says something about sexual molestation, and consequences occur, the story starts to change. Anyone who has worked with child abuse for any length of time knows that that's a very common phenomenon.

Mr. Monk: How significant were the statements made by Katherine, the statements that appear throughout the reports that "my mommy taught me this"? Were they significant to you?

Dr. Carrier: Yes, they were. Sexual behavior in children this young is learned from the parents.

Mr. Monk: Is it your professional opinion, Doctor, that this child learned her sexual behavior from her mother?

Dr. Carrier: I would say so, in my opinion, yes.

Mr. Monk: Would you say that Katherine's total denial of ever having told anyone about the molestation is indicative that she is under some pressure to change her story?

Dr. Carrier: I would say so, yes.

Mr. Monk: Did she exhibit that pressure?

Dr. Carrier: She exhibited that pressure by being anxious with me.

Mr. Monk: Do you have an opinion as to the source of that pressure?

Dr. Carrier: Yes, I do.

Mr. Monk: What is your opinion?

Dr. Carrier: My opinion is that the pressure is from her mother.

Mr. Monk: Assuming you are right, do you think that the mother, by asking that the child not tell the truth, is acting in the child's best interests?

Dr. Carrier: No, I don't.

Mr. Monk: Doctor, based on what you have discovered about the dynamics of mother-daughter incest, and remembering what you know of Katherine and her background, do you think that it is in her psychological best interests for her environment to be controlled?

Dr. Carrier: Yes, I do.

Mr. Monk: Is it in Katherine's best psychological interests that she be removed from her mother's custody?

Dr. Carrier: Yes, it is.

Mr. Monk: Thank you. Nothing further.

The Court: Ms. Douglas, recross?

Ms. Douglas: Very, very briefly.

Ms. Douglas: Would your opinion change, Doctor, if you now found out that, in fact, Ms. Cross volunteered to take a psychological examination and signed a release of information for the Child Protective Services—including yourself—to contact her current therapist and see any records available?

Dr. Carrier: Would I change my opinion about removing the child from the home? Is that what you are asking?

Ms. Douglas: Yes.

Dr. Carrier: Not entirely, because I think the risk is too high.

Ms. Douglas: But, earlier today, you stated, that a couple issues needed to be addressed before that determination could be made. Is that correct?

Dr. Carrier: That's correct.

Ms. Douglas: And those issues were whether Katherine and Helen Cross would get proper treatment.

Dr. Carrier: (No audible response.)

Ms. Douglas: Dr. Carrier?

Dr. Carrier: Yeah. Oh, yeah. Okay.

Ms. Douglas: Your concerns were whether Katherine would get proper treatment given her mother's resistance. Correct?

Dr. Carrier: Yes.

Ms. Douglas: You stated that you had been informed that the mother refused to take a psychological examination and she refused to sign the release of information for Child Protective Services? If those facts were incorrect, but the opposite was true, are you now stating that it still wouldn't change your opinion?

Dr. Carrier: I didn't say it wouldn't, I said not entirely, I be-

lieve is what I said. If that is, in fact, true, that she had volunteered to take a psychological evaluation, and given
blanket access to any and all therapists, then it would tem-
per my opinion.

Ms. Douglas: Dr. Carrier. Can you remind us who told you
that she refused to be evaluated?

Dr. Carrier: It was Matt Bickel.

Ms. Douglas: Thank you, Doctor. No further questions.

The Court: Ms. Escobar?

Ms. Escobar: I have no further questions of this witness,
Your Honor.

The Court: Doctor, you are excused then. However, I would
like to offer you the same courtesy that we've offered Dr.
Abramson. That is, if it would interest you, please feel free
to remain for the rest of the trial.

Dr. Carrier: I would appreciate that, thank you.

The Court: Very good.

At this point, with an exaggerated gesture, Dr. Carrier
looked at his watch. With his hand on his forehead, he tilted
back, rolled his eyes, and said, a bit too loudly, "Oh no, I
have another appointment. May I be excused?" After being
formally excused by Judge Shriver, Dr. Carrier speedily col-
lected his papers and left the courthouse. Peering out the
courtroom window, I could see him racing away in his Ca-
maro, sand and dust drifting in his wake.

Dr. Carrier's rapid departure surprised all of us, including
Judge Shriver, who, looking slightly flustered, called a brief
recess.

When the trial resumed the prosecution called to the
stand Dr. Nancy Dworkin, the pediatrician who examined
Katherine for signs of sexual abuse. Dr. Dworkin was expected to testify (as in her report) that she found evidence
consistent with the possibility of molestation.

Mr. Monk: Dr. Dworkin, on or about June of this year, were
you working for the Department of Mental Health at Mendocino General Hospital?

Dr. Dworkin: Yes, I was.

Mr. Monk: In what capacity?

Dr. Dworkin: I'm a pediatrician and medical director of the
Child Abuse and Neglect Team of Mendocino General Hospital. I was working that morning in the Outpatient Clinic.

Mr. Monk: On July 5, 1997, did you examine Katherine
Cross?

Dr. Dworkin: Yes, I conducted a physical examination of her.

Mr. Monk: And what was the reason for this examination?

Dr. Dworkin: Well, it's a standard procedure in children that
are referred to the clinic for suspected child abuse.

Mr. Monk: Did you examine her to see whether or not there
was any physical evidence of sexual abuse?

Dr. Dworkin: Yes, I did.

Mr. Monk: And did you find any?

Dr. Dworkin: I found physical evidence that would be consistent with molestation.

Mr. Monk: You said in your report that there is no definite
physical evidence of vaginal or anal penetration?

Dr. Dworkin: Yes.

Mr. Monk: How do you square this sentence in your report with the last one you have just made; that is, you found symptoms consistent with an explanation of sexual abuse?

Dr. Dworkin: The two major findings during the examination, the redness and thickening of the skin overlying the labia majora, are unusual in a healthy young child. Since sexual fondling can produce those changes, I believe that the physical findings are consistent with sexual molestation.

Mr. Monk: Were you able to determine the specific cause of these physical conditions?

Dr. Dworkin: No.

Mr. Monk: Did you ask the child any questions about it?

Dr. Dworkin: No.

Mr. Monk: Did she volunteer any statements?

Dr. Dworkin: No.

Mr. Monk: You say in your report that you found no actual anal or vaginal penetration?

Dr. Dworkin: That is correct. I did not find any physical evidence that there had been vaginal or anal penetration. Generally, you are looking for an enlarged vaginal opening or for evidence of scarring to the hymenal ring. Also, an enlarged opening or thinning of that membrane in the anal exam. None of those findings were present in this girl.

Mr. Monk: Is it your job to determine whether or not the child you are examining is a victim of sexual abuse?

Dr. Dworkin: Yes.

Mr. Monk: And your opinion in this case?

Dr. Dworkin: What I stated in my report was that the pig-

mentation in the inner labia is consistent with sexual molestation. However, there is no definite physical evidence of
vaginal or anal penetration.

Mr. Monk: Would you read your last sentence?

Dr. Dworkin [reading]: She had quite an abnormal response
to this examination. That would indicate previous sexual experience.

Mr. Monk: What made you write that?

Dr. Dworkin: When Katherine came to the clinic, she was
fairly cheerful and giggly throughout the general physical examination, which we performed as part of the evaluation.
When it came to examining her genitalia—her vagina and
her rectum—she initially was hesitant, as many children are.
But, then, after some urging, and working with myself and
the nurse who helps me with these examinations, she became very compliant. She laid back and spread her legs and
then, throughout the whole genital examination continued
to giggle, which I found distinctly abnormal. That is an unusual response for a girl. And my interpretation is that she
had previous sexual experience with people looking at her
genitalia.

Mr. Monk: Is it your job, after you have made your examination, to submit your evaluation to some agency?

Dr. Dworkin: If the child is brought in by Child Protective
Services or law enforcement agencies, I'll send them a copy
of the report that I write. If a parent brings in the child, or a
physician refers the child in, then I'll send a report to that
person.

Mr. Monk: Doctor, in the last sentence of your report, you
say it is quite an abnormal response. Is there a reason why

you said "quite an abnormal response," as opposed to merely "an abnormal response"?

Dr. Dworkin: I've never had a young girl giggle throughout the whole examination.

Mr. Monk: How long have you been conducting genital exams on children?

Dr. Dworkin: As a pediatrician, I've been examining children since 1975.

Mr. Monk: Have you ever seen a girl act like this?

Dr. Dworkin: No.

Mr. Monk: Thank you, Doctor. Nothing further.

The Court: Ms. Douglas.

Ms. Douglas: Thank you, Your Honor.

Dr. Dworkin's report was, potentially, the most damaging evidence against Helen Cross. As a respected pediatrician, Dr. Dworkin's testimony that she had found physical evidence consistent with molestation was certain to influence the judge. Megan's objective in her cross-examination was to disarm the doctor's findings by introducing a plausible alternative to the molestation interpretation, and failing that, to raise the possibility of a perpetrator other than Helen.

Ms. Douglas: Prior to the physical examination, were you given any documents to read or were you supplied with any information about Katherine Cross?

Dr. Dworkin: Yes, I was.

Ms. Douglas: And what information was that?

Dr. Dworkin: I just made some notes from a conversation I had with Matt Bickel, the social worker from CPS.

Ms. Douglas: Did you receive information from anyone other than Matt Bickel?

Dr. Dworkin: No, I didn't.

Ms. Douglas: Can you be more specific about the information that you received from Mr. Bickel?

Dr. Dworkin: He said that this child was in protective custody, and there were allegations about possible sexual abuse.

Ms. Douglas: So you were specifically looking for signs of sexual abuse?

Dr. Dworkin: Yes. I examined the child for signs of sexual abuse.

Ms. Douglas: Thank you, Doctor. Your report speaks of generalized and mild erythema. Is that "redness"?

Dr. Dworkin: Yes.

Ms. Douglas: Can this erythema be produced as a result of irritation, infection, friction from clothing, allergies to clothing or dye?

Dr. Dworkin: Yes, it can.

Ms. Douglas: Can you explain what Neosporin is?

Dr. Dworkin: It's an ointment, an antibiotic, that is commonly used to treat skin infections.

Ms. Douglas: If Neosporin is applied to skin that is sensitive to it, could the skin become reddened, with swelling and itching?

Dr. Dworkin: Yes.

Ms. Douglas: If Neosporin is applied inappropriately, could it create hyperpigmentation and external erythema?

Dr. Dworkin: Yes. If the person is sensitive or allergic to Neosporin.

Ms. Douglas: Could your findings from the examination of Katherine Cross be consistent with anything other than sexual molestation?

Dr. Dworkin: Which findings are you referring to?

Ms. Douglas: The physical findings, the erythema, the hyperpigmentation, the thickening of the labia.

Dr. Dworkin: Yes.

Ms. Douglas: Also, Doctor, during your examination, I believe you stated that the hymen was intact. There was an opening of six millimeters, or about a quarter of an inch. Is that correct?

Dr. Dworkin: Yes.

Ms. Douglas: Does that indicate that no vaginal penetration occurred?

Dr. Dworkin: Yes. There was no traumatic penetration by anything larger than six millimeters.

Ms. Douglas: That's about the size of a moistened Q-Tip you said in your report?

Dr. Dworkin: Yes.

Ms. Douglas: Nothing further.

The Court: Ms. Escobar.

Ms. Escobar: Doctor, you have indicated that Katherine giggled through the examination.

Dr. Dworkin: Yes.

Ms. Escobar: Were any efforts made on the part of yourself or your nurse to make the examination less stressful for her?

Dr. Dworkin: We tried. We try to make every examination nonstressful.

Ms. Escobar: Did she appear to be stressed?

Dr. Dworkin: Well, it's conceivable the giggling was her way of dealing with stress.

Ms. Escobar: Do some people giggle inappropriately when they are stressed?

Dr. Dworkin: Yes.

Ms. Escobar: Thank you. No further questions.

Monk made one last attempt at salvaging this witness in his redirect examination. Here he again tried to characterize Katherine's masturbation as "excessive" and thereby to infer that she was exhibiting anomalous behavior in need of explanation. His explanation, of course, was that she had been molested by her mother.

The Court: Redirect?

Mr. Monk: Yes, Your Honor.

Doctor, in your opinion, is there such a thing as excessive masturbation for a child that age?

Dr. Dworkin: Yes.

Mr. Monk: Were the results you found consistent with this excessive masturbation?

Dr. Dworkin: Yes.

Mr. Monk: When would masturbation be excessive for a girl that age?

Dr. Dworkin: When it caused injury or other physical problems.

Mr. Monk: Did you see symptoms in her diagnosis consistent with excessive masturbation?

Dr. Dworkin: Yes, I do.

This partially contradicts Dr. Dworkin's earlier testimony, in which she concluded that the labial thickening was from molestation. Masturbation is another reasonable explanation for her findings—one which, up to this point, she had been unwilling to acknowledge.

Mr. Monk: Is it uncommon for a five-year-old girl to masturbate in public school?

Ms. Douglas: Objection. Dr. Dworkin is not an expert on human sexuality.

The Court: Sustained.

Mr. Monk: Nothing further, Your Honor.

The Court: You are excused, Doctor. Thank you.

It was a little past noon, and time for a break, so Judge Shriver called for a recess and asked that all parties return to the courthouse at 1:30 sharp.

Megan wanted me to join her for lunch at a local fish shack. I told her that I'd catch up with her, but I wanted to review my notes first. Particularly Bickel's interview with the Lopeses.

Mary Lopes was scheduled to testify for the prosecution next. From my vantage point, Monk was losing the case, and he knew it. Undoubtedly, he had at least one more card up his sleeve. Perhaps he would revisit Helen's "sexual indiscretions" and try somehow to tie her behavior to either Katherine, or other children. In order to properly sully Helen's reputation, he needed Mary Lopes to testify.

When Bickel had interviewed her, Lopes told him some rather sordid tales about Helen's sex life, many of which I knew to be true, and others of which were probably complete fabrications. I decided to reread the interview to prepare for the coming onslaught. When I did, I discovered something curious, and more than a little suspicious, that I hadn't noticed previously—a page was missing! The interview with Lopes ended on page 23, but the next interview didn't begin until page 25. *What happened to page 24?*

In retrospect, it was not all that surprising that neither I nor Megan had noticed the discrepancy on previous readings. The Lopes interview appears to terminate quite sufficiently, without a half sentence or a half paragraph in evidence. Of course, there might be no relevance to the missing page. The error itself might have been inadvertent. Perhaps coffee was spilled on it and the page was discarded. Or, maybe the page got jammed in the copying machine and was never printed. These possibilities notwithstanding, the absence of page 24 in a document with otherwise consecutive pages had become glaringly conspicuous. Moreover, because these were Bickel's notes, my suspicions were heightened.

I needed to find Megan. As expected, I found her slicing through a hunk of freshly smoked Pacific salmon at a local smokehouse restaurant. When I told her what I had discovered, she dropped her fork in excitement. "We've got to get down to CPS and take a look at the originals!" she exclaimed. Because Bickel and Osborn were liable to be at lunch, we might get lucky and only need to convince a receptionist that handing over the records was an appropriate course of action. A receptionist would have no vested interest in this case, and might show us the "entire" file, page 24 and all.

We got lucky. The receptionist was easily distracted with

small talk about her children's "Santa pictures," which were clearly visible behind the front desk. Using her most charming voice and demeanor, Megan told her, "I represent Helen Cross. I subpoenaed her records, and your office sent me this" (showing the receptionist our existing file). "I just noticed a page was missing. Probably got stuck in the Xerox machine. Could you recopy page 24 for me? Here's the original subpoena."

The receptionist took a cursory look at the subpoena. Smiling, and apologizing for the error, she went down a corridor and entered an office. After hearing her shut a file drawer, we saw her reappear in the corridor, carrying a single page. She walked directly to the copier, made a copy, and came back to us. Then, to our delight and astonishment, she handed us page 24! We thanked her and quickly exited the building.

When we got to my car and read the "missing" page, we were shocked and thrilled with what we had discovered. Mary Lopes clearly thought Bickel considered her and her husband potential suspects in the sexual abuse of Katherine Cross. When Bickel questioned her, she was very defensive and seemed to be hiding something. Here's how the interview ended, as reconstructed from Bickel's notes on page 24:

> **Bickel:** If we're going to use you, I need to know, have you ever touched Katherine Cross in the genital area?
>
> **Lopes:** No. Did Katie say that? Well, she must have been talking about when I wiped her after she went to the bathroom. Is that what it was? Because I never—John might have—but I never touched her like that. Sexually, I mean.

Bickel: I didn't say she accused you of anything. But I need to know, have you or your husband ever touched Katherine Cross in the genital area?

Lopes: No, I said I didn't. But if you have some kind of evidence about John, I want to know what it is. I told him to stay away from her! If that bastard touched her I'll kill him! Did he? 'Cause I'll send him back to prison.

Bickel: Look, I didn't say either of you did anything, I'm just asking.

Lopes: I don't think I should answer any more questions without my lawyer.

This concluded the interview.

After reading this, Megan exclaimed, "Wow! When Monk brings Lopes to the stand, we've got them! I'll hang her—and Bickel, for leaving this out. Of course he'll just claim that the omission was inadvertent, but it will raise suspicions about him to the judge. All I need to do is to get Lopes to start acting crazy to diminish the value of her testimony. Who knows, she might even confess! Maybe I'll just ask her to explain her comments from this interview."

We rushed back to the courthouse, making the 1:30 deadline. Dave Monk was standing before the bench. The judge turned to him and asked:

The Court: Do you have another witness, Mr. Monk?

Mr. Monk: Yes, Your Honor. My next witness is Mrs. Mary Lopes.

At this, the judge raised his eyebrows slightly and asked the attorneys to approach the bench. (After the trial concluded, Judge Shriver confided to me that he was horrified to see Mary Lopes in his courtroom, particularly because it was at the request of Child Protective Services and County Counsel. Judge Shriver told me, "We tried Mary and her husband John for molesting their own kids, both the boy and the girl. Only the husband was convicted. I'll always remember him as a sick individual, especially his testimony that 'infants should be licked clean after urinating.' He was very disturbed, and I had my doubts about her too. I can't believe they called her as a witness!")

The Court: Mr. Monk, what is the purpose of this witness?

Mr. Monk: It's about the Oreo cookie I mentioned earlier.

The Court: I have already warned you that inappropriate slang has no place in this courtroom.

Mr. Monk: I am sorry, Your Honor. What I meant to say is that this witness will give testimony about Helen Cross's sexual perversions.

The Court: I have made it very clear that Ms. Cross's sexual behavior has no bearing on this case—unless you are presenting testimony about her sexual contact with children. And I am adamant about this. If I hear any further comments about *ménage à trois* with other adults, or any other adult sexual behavior, I will excuse your witness and strike her testimony from the record. Is that clear?

Mr. Monk: Yes, Your Honor.

The Court: Is there any reason, then, that this witness should testify in this matter?

Mr. Monk: Yes, Your Honor. She can talk about what she observed Katherine Cross do with her children.

The Court: If you limit your questions to that arena, I will allow her testimony.

Mr. Monk: Yes, I will. And thank you, Your Honor.

Mr. Monk: Mrs. Lopes, approximately how long have you known Helen Cross?

Mrs. Lopes: About four or five years.

Mr. Monk: Did you ever have reason to confront her and tell her that her child was acting sexually inappropriate?

Mrs. Lopes: I did confront her, last February or March.

Mr. Monk: What did that confrontation consist of?

Mrs. Lopes: There had been an incident in the schoolyard, and I mentioned two previous ones that I felt were bothering me.

Mr. Monk: Did you directly observe those two previous incidents?

Mrs. Lopes: Yes.

Mr. Monk: When was the first?

Mrs. Lopes: The first one was the previous summer. There was another lady living with us, and she called my attention to what was happening on the porch, and it was with my two kids and Katie.

Mr. Monk: By Katie, you mean Katherine Cross?

Mrs. Lopes: Yes.

Mr. Monk: What did you see?

Mrs. Lopes: Katie was directing Beth to be a boy and she would lie down in the middle, between her and Ben.

Mr. Monk: Beth and Ben are your children?

Mrs. Lopes: Yes.

Mr. Monk: What was the second incident?

Mrs. Lopes: The second incident was in the fall of '95. When I walked into the kids' bedroom, Katie was holding dolls and telling Ben the one doll should put its face down on the other doll.

Mr. Monk: You mean the private parts?

Mrs. Lopes: Private parts, yes. On it. And perhaps I overreacted. But I asked them to come out to the living room and watch television until Katie's mommy got home.

Mr. Monk: This was the fall of 1995?

Mrs. Lopes: Uh-huh.

Mr. Monk: Why do you say perhaps you overreacted?

Mrs. Lopes: Because I had just been through a situation like this myself.

Mr. Monk: When you say "a situation like this," what do you mean?

Mrs. Lopes: I was on trial, with my husband. And I was trying to protect my children. And, well, I didn't tell Helen, but I did try to protect my own children.

Mr. Monk: Were you yourself on trial facing allegations of child abuse?

Mrs. Lopes: Yes, I was.

Mr. Monk: When the incident happened, did you talk to Katherine about it?

Mrs. Lopes: I let her know that it wasn't acceptable behavior. We took them out to watch television and then, within a few minutes, she was doing it again. I made her stop it.

Mr. Monk: Did Helen come and pick up the child?

Mrs. Lopes: Yes. *Several* hours later.

Mr. Monk: Did you say anything to Helen Cross?

Mrs. Lopes: Yes. But she didn't seem to care.

Mr. Monk: What was the third incident?

Mrs. Lopes: The third incident was the one last February or March. I was driving by their school, and I saw my daughter, Beth, forcing her skirt down and looking terrified. So, when I picked her up from school, I asked her to tell me what happened. And she became hysterical and said that Katie . . .

Ms. Douglas: Objection. Hearsay.

The Court: Sustained.

Mr. Monk: Okay. Mrs. Lopes, when did you confront Helen about this incident?

Mrs. Lopes: That night. I told her what I'd seen in the play yard. I asked Beth and Katie to go in another room so we can discuss them privately.

Mr. Monk: Did you inform her of the facts of the incident?

Mrs. Lopes: Yes. But she didn't care then either.

This testimony was an out-and-out lie. This was the first that Helen had heard of any of the three incidents to which Lopes referred.

Mr. Monk: Did you ever inform the school about these incidents?

Mrs. Lopes: Yes, I did.

Mr. Monk: When was that?

Mrs. Lopes: Two days later.

Mr. Monk: And was this teacher the only person to whom you conveyed this information?

Mrs. Lopes: No. I talked to my counsel.

Mr. Monk: Why did you speak to your counsel about it?

Mrs. Lopes: Because of everything me and my husband had been through over the last couple of months.

Mr. Monk: And why did you inform the school?

Mrs. Lopes: Because I wanted something done about this problem.

Mr. Monk: No further questions.

The Court: Thank you. Your witness, Ms. Douglas.

Ms. Douglas: Do you know who Matt Bickel is?

Mrs. Lopes: Yes. He works for Child Protective Services.

Ms. Douglas: Did he interview you and your husband about the allegations in this case?

Mrs. Lopes: Yes, he did.

Ms. Douglas: I want to ask you some questions about that interview.

Mrs. Lopes: Okay.

Ms. Douglas [addressing the court]: Before doing so, however, I want to introduce a missing page from that interview. Your Honor, if you will look at exhibit E, you will notice that there is a page 22, 23, 25, 26, and so forth. But there's no page 24—it's missing. I just noticed this, and obtained the missing page from CPS. Thus, I would like to add page 24 to Exhibit E, and ask this witness questions about it.

Mr. Monk: Your Honor, I would also like to see this. Page 24 is missing from my Exhibit E as well.

As this episode began to unfold, Bickel turned bright red and beads of sweat began to appear on his darkening forehead. Osborn turned to him and asked, "What the hell's going on?" Bickel shrugged his shoulders, and said, "I really don't know what page they're talking about. We gave them all the records."

Osborn then stepped forward to read the page with the prosecutor, Monk. Within seconds, both of them looked distraught. Almost simultaneously, they looked back at Bickel, who sat stonefaced, ignoring their glances.

Mr. Monk [addressing the Court]: How do we know that this is from the same interview with the Lopeses?

The Court: It has the same ID number, and date, as the preceding and following pages. The handwriting looks the same, and it contains that same interviewer name, Mr. Bickel, as well as the Lopeses. And unless Mr. Bickel is now going to claim this is not his handwriting or his interview, I will consider it part of the original Exhibit E.

Mr. Bickel [standing and answering in a very subdued manner]: It is part of that interview, Your Honor.

The Court: Ms. Douglas, you can continue.

Ms. Douglas: Mrs. Lopes, let me read you something from this interview: "Well she must have been talking about when I wiped her." Did you say that?

Mrs. Lopes [with tears welling up in her eyes]: Yeah, I said it. But I only wiped her. It wasn't a sexual thing. It wasn't . . . It was just good hygiene. You gotta do that with kids.

Ms. Douglas: Which means that you touched her genitals?

Mrs. Lopes [crying]: Yeah. But it wasn't a sexual thing. I didn't do anything sexual. You gotta believe me. I'm not like John. I don't know what he did. But I don't do sexual things with kids.

Megan looked, in turn, at both Judge Shriver and Mr. Monk. Then she raised her eyebrows and sighed audibly.

Ms. Douglas: Your Honor, I have nothing more to ask this witness.

The Court: Mr. Monk?

Mr. Monk: Uh, no, Your Honor.

The Court: Well, I believe that wraps it up for today. The Court will hear closing arguments Monday morning at 8:00.

Minutes later, Monk, Osborn, and Bickel could be heard arguing heatedly in the back of the courtroom. I couldn't make out their exact words, but it was clear that Monk wanted to know the truth about the missing page, and seemed to be accusing Bickel. Monk wasn't alone—we all wanted to know what had happened to page 24 and what could possibly have compelled Bickel to try to hide this crucial evidence. Megan and I would soon find out.

THE INSIDE SCOOP
ON MR. MATT BICKEL

Minutes after Judge Shriver had dismissed the courtroom, Megan was on her cellular phone calling her office and arranging to have a private detective look into Bickel's background. We didn't know what to expect, but we were confident that he would turn up something. The main question was, when? We needed the information as soon as possible, and by Sunday evening at the latest.

As it turned out, we didn't need to wait long. On Saturday afternoon, the private investigator provided us with a brief summary of Bickel's life and copies of essential records. Suddenly, the puzzle pieces began to fit.

I had long wondered why Child Protective Services wanted to prosecute Helen when neither the district attorney nor County Counsel initially believed that the case was worth pursuing. The answer, as it turned out, was Matt Bickel, a recently hired CPS case worker. His motives were a unique combination of youth, professional ambition, and unresolved psychological issues.

Bickel was twenty-one years old when the Cross case began, with a bachelor's degree in sociology from Humbolt State University. He held no advanced degrees, nor had he undergone the additional training in psychology and social work needed to prepare him for his position with CPS. Bickel was in over his head, but failed to realize it. He was happy just to have a job.

Indeed, the Mendocino County budget had allocated

funds for only a half-time position, although CPS desired a
full-time employee, hence expected a full-time commitment
from Bickel. He was glad for the opportunity, and content
with the salary. In a just world, he would never be assigned
to his position, based upon his age, experience, and job
training. Too much was at stake, as the name of the
agency—Child Protective Services—makes clear.

Unfortunately, Bickel was neither skilled enough, nor per-
ceptive enough, to recognize his own limitations and biases.
As such, he was both unable and unwilling to cast a wider
net when investigating the roots of Katherine's conduct. Instead he focused solely on Helen, whom he pursued with a
vengeance.

In retrospect, it is clear that Bickel was attempting to ex-
orcise his own demons by prosecuting Helen. As the records
provided by the private detective indicated, Bickel was born
to a heroin-addicted prostitute, who was later arrested and
convicted of bank robbery. After the conviction, when he
was only two years old, Bickel was removed from his
mother's custody and made a ward of the state. Because
Bickel's father had deserted him before birth, and no other
biological relative came forward to serve as his guardian,
Bickel was sent to a foster home, where he spent two years
before eventually being adopted. However, he continued to
harbor rage and resentment toward his mother, which (we
surmise) he may have projected onto Helen Cross. Like
Bickel's own mother, Helen was not married to Katherine's
father. And like his own mother, Helen was accused of sexual improprieties.

This time, Bickel was not going to let "her" get away,
even if it meant excluding critical suspects (such as the

Lopeses) from his investigations and final report. However, Bickel wasn't acting alone, as a one-man lynch mob. All he did was to amplify the concerns and suspicions of the CPS experts, including Dr. Carrier and Dr. Dworkin. The evidence, such as it was, did stack up against Helen. The police believed that Helen was guilty, as did Marcia Osborn, Bickel's CPS supervisor. And Drs. Carrier and Dworkin both believed it as well. Bickel didn't create these suspicions, but he did enflame them to new heights.

Much later that evening, Megan and I returned to her Mendocino "office" (a suite at the Heritage House hotel) to discuss her closing statement. After hammering out the details, and debating the pros and cons of various strategies, we turned our attention to the Lopes discovery, and Bickel's complicity. The task for Megan Douglas was to subtly raise these issues in her closing statement. She needed to convince the judge that Bickel was both arbitrary and persecutory in the manner in which he investigated the case. And, as a result of his arbitrariness, he may have let the real perpetrator—if there was one—escape. All that was needed was to convince the judge of the weakness of the case against Helen, which would never have been pursued if it weren't for Bickel's personal vendetta.

THE TRIAL: DAY THREE

The Court: The Court will now hear concluding statements in the Cross case.

Ms. Douglas?

Ms. Douglas: Your Honor, at this time, I would like the Court to dismiss the allegations. I don't believe that there has been sufficient showing on part of Child Protective Services to demonstrate that Helen Cross is not capable of, willing to, or actually exercising proper care, custody, and control. I don't believe they had met their burden that this child is a victim of sexual abuse of her mother, or that if the child is a victim of sexual abuse of someone else, that the mother failed to protect. Clearly, by putting her daughter in therapy, Helen Cross was acting as a responsible parent.

We've heard expert testimony that if a parent becomes aware of inappropriate behavior, the proper course of action is therapy. The record clearly reflects that the mother put her child in treatment. I believe the record also reflects the child continues to be in psychotherapy. I don't believe there is anywhere close to being sufficient evidence to show this mother may have molested the child. If the child was molested, there are other potential perpetrators in her social network, which have been denied or overlooked by both the police and Child Protective Services. The investigation, in fact, has been a travesty, Your Honor. It is quite clear that the investigation of and case against my client were motivated by factors other than a concern for the welfare of the

child. In short, there is absolutely no compelling evidence
that Helen Cross sexually molested her daughter. Quite the
opposite. She is a devoted, caring mother, who has always
put her daughter's best interests first. On that basis, I ask
the Court to dismiss the petition at this time.

Just as Megan completed her closing argument, a furious
scream was heard from the back of the courtroom. "You
fucking liar! You bitch! Don't listen to her!"

The screaming was coming from Bickel, who was kicking
chairs aside as he made his way toward Megan. The shock
of this outrageous scene temporarily immobilized everyone
else in the courtroom. Fortunately, two sheriffs overheard
the scream while sitting in their trailer, a few hundred feet
away. They ran over, burst into the room, and lunged toward Bickel. A third sheriff raced in front of the judge, with
his weapon drawn. Bickel was dragged from the courtroom,
screaming incoherently.

Prior to this incident, Bickel had been the model of courtroom decorum. He was well dressed, polite, and sat quietly
throughout the proceedings, even through the previous day's
bizarre twists and turns. In fact, his modest and understated
demeanor made his outburst especially frightening. (Shortly
after the trial concluded, Bickel was terminated by Child
Protective Services. In a small town like Mendocino, ranting
and raving are best done in private. After his well-publicized
outburst in the courtroom, no one was willing to take a
chance on Bickel's psychological stability by offering him a
job. He left town shortly thereafter.)

When we regained our composure and order was restored to the courtroom, Megan handed Judge Shriver the documents we had received on Bickel's background, such as his foster home records. Megan said, "These may help explain Mr. Bickel's outburst." The judge glanced at the papers quickly and then put the documents to the side, saying, "Thank you Ms. Douglas. I believe they might."

After a delay of nearly half an hour, Judge Shriver reconvened the court, minus the disruptive presence of Matt Bickel. Monk was visibly shaken by the disturbing turn of events that had just transpired.

The Court: Mr. Monk, do you feel you can continue at this time?

Mr. Monk: Yes, Your Honor.

The Court: Please proceed.

Mr. Monk: Dr. Dworkin, Dr. Carrier, and in particular, CPS, have gathered evidence and submitted reports, unequivocally stating that this child has been the victim of sexual abuse by her mother. And, Your Honor, I shall rest my case on the total of that information, both documentary and oral, and submit it to the Court.

The Court: Ms. Escobar?

Ms. Escobar: Your Honor, I don't believe that there is sufficient evidence that the petition is true in any aspect. I think that, perhaps, medication was applied inappropriately. I don't think at this point the Court can find that there has been sexual abuse, or failure to protect, by the mother. In short, I don't believe that Child Protective Services have met their burden, and I would ask the Court to dismiss the case.

The Court: Ms. Douglas, anything further?

Ms. Douglas: Only two further points, Your Honor. First, the evidence presented by Dr. Dworkin is now especially problematic in light of the testimony of Mrs. Lopes. Even if physical evidence of molestation were present, there are other potential perpetrators. And second, there is no evidence, whatsoever, that the child is sexually acting out at the present. The most recent record of any problem is many months ago, maybe six or eight. I don't believe that there is evidence showing that there is a present problem which requires court dependency.

The Court: The Court will take a brief recess to review the psychological reports and some of the other documents.

This was the moment of judgment. Soon Helen Cross would know whether she would lose Katherine or whether she could take her daughter home and begin rebuilding their lives. The tension in the courtroom and in the wooded grove outside, where Marcia Osborn and Dave Monk had gone to smoke, was extraordinary. Helen was shaking silently, tears flowing from her eyes, as she sat awaiting the judge's decision. Her words, in contrast, were optimistic and hopeful: "I think we convinced him. And what about that crazy Matt Bickel? That will help, right?" Helen repeated several variations on this theme, more to reassure herself than to solicit answers from others.

We all hoped that she was right—that the Bickel scene and Mary Lopes's bizarre denials might benefit our side, if only by raising suspicions about Bickel's report and introducing additional suspects. A solid, painful hour passed before Judge Shriver returned from his chambers.

The Court: We'll recall the Cross matter. The Court, in examining the Petition itself, notes that we have to deal with a number of issues.

First, the Petition, in Paragraph one, states that said minor has been or was sexually acting out inappropriately. That does not seem to be in dispute by any of the parties, and the Court certainly finds that is true.

Has the child been either molested or exposed to sexual activity or conduct which was inappropriate? Dr. Carrier believes so; Dr. Abramson says it is unlikely. Dr. Dworkin says possibly. This Court feels that it is possible, though not certain, that Katherine Cross has been exposed to some kind of sexual trauma or behavior that was inappropriate, and that it has caused her, at least in part, to act out sexually in an inappropriate manner. That exposure, and the resultant acting out certainly warrants therapy, and certainly warrants actions by the parents or other responsible parties.

Was the minor exposed to that sexual activity by the mother, or if not by the mother, did the mother fail to protect the child? Assuming for a moment that the mother did not molest the child, that the exposure to sexual activity was by other parties or persons or parties unknown, the Court cannot find that the mother failed to protect. However, testimony heard in this courtroom would lead me to admonish the mother to be more vigilant in selecting potential caretakers for her child.

The Court does feel that when the matter was brought to the mother that she took the appropriate steps. That is, getting the child to counseling, and herself as well. So then we have to return to whether or not the mother is, in fact, the person who molested the child.

The Court feels that the evidence does not support such a conclusion. The demonstration by Dr. Abramson of the child's inability to distinguish between the prepositions "in" and "on," together with other evidence presented in his report and testimony casts doubt upon the veracity of the child's testimony. Moreover, sufficient doubt has been raised in this courtroom regarding the veracity of the ancillary evidence presented in support of the charges against the mother. The ultimate source of much of this information, Child Protective Services, has been largely discredited.

Finally, the evidence also does not support the allegation that the mother exposed her child to inappropriate sexual activity. Instead, as mentioned, when confronted with these issues, the mother placed the child into therapy. She has also experienced the trauma that the removal of a child can cause—and the family relationship has been severely jeopardized.

This Court, based upon the evidence that it has, cannot conclude that Helen Cross is not exercising proper and effective parental care and control, and cannot find that her home is unfit. She has obviously taken steps to assure the child's safety, and to assure the child's emotional well-being. So, the Court orders this matter dismissed.

Upon hearing this proclamation, Megan smiled broadly and gave me a life-threatening bear hug. We had won! Helen and Katherine would be reunited, for good.

But Helen didn't join our impromptu celebration. Instead, she remained seated in the wooden chair she had occupied throughout the trial, the exhaustion evident in her vacuous stare. Several minutes elapsed before she spoke.

"So it's finally over?" she asked me quietly.

"Yes," I told her, "it's over, and you won."

"Did I, Paul?"

Her vacant cast suggested that for Helen, the conclusion of the trial was as unreal as its beginning. How could she have been accused of such a thing? And what would she do now?

After a long silence, Helen arose and hugged me, tears streaming down her pale face. Moments later, Julia took Helen by the hand and led her out of the courtroom. Together they drove to the babysitter's, to reclaim Helen's daughter.

AFTERMATH

As I was leaving the courtroom, Judge Shriver summoned me to the bench, inciting my curiosity. The judge, who is a tall man (6´4˝ at least) with dark black hair, stood up and smiled. After hesitating for a moment, he asked me if I would like to join him for dinner, if I didn't already have other plans. Flattered, I quickly answered, "I'd be honored" (the pun, of course, was entirely unintentional).

We left in the judge's car, a new Range Rover, the high end of Jeep culture. When we arrived at the Cafe Beaujolais, thought by many to be Mendocino's finest restaurant, we were greeted by a betuxed *maître d'* who immediately recognized the judge and escorted us to his favorite table (which, inexplicably, was near the kitchen). Without glancing at the menu, Judge Shriver ordered a spit-roasted duck with grilled radicchio and a bottle of chardonnay from *North Coast Estates*, a local Mendocino County winery. I took a few moments to examine the offerings and then followed suit, selecting the seared sea scallops with gremolata.

After the drinks were served and a few pleasantries exchanged, we began our post-trial analysis. Not surprisingly, most of the talk focused on the peculiar events surrounding Matt Bickel's unraveling and the Lopeses' involvement. Since the judge had not had time to read all of the documents on Bickel that Megan had given to him, I briefly filled him in: "All I know is from what I have read in those reports and records. Apparently, Bickel's mother was a heroin-addicted prostitute who was jailed for bank robbery. Bickel was shuffled from foster home to foster home, usually with poor results. He had great difficulty with parental figures, especially women. And he was angry as hell. Yet, around high school, he quieted down and kept to himself. Maybe this was how he plotted his revenge—work for Child Protective Services and rid the world of bad mothers. Or maybe it was kismet of the blackest kind."

"It's funny," the judge replied, "he never seemed bitter, merely reserved, until his outburst today. His demeanor never betrayed all that inner turmoil. I guess his quietness hid a lot."

After a moment's silence for further wine tasting, Judge Shriver added, "I never thought he was qualified for his position at CPS. Now it's clear that he wasn't emotionally fit either. I guess that's what happens when you try to operate a service agency on a shoestring. It's a shame—these are people's lives we're playing around with. Who knows what damage this ordeal has done to Ms. Cross and her daughter."

"And then there's the Lopes fiasco," he continued. "If you ask me, they should have hauled John Lopes's ass in for questioning. Then, to call Mary Lopes as a witness! What was the prosecution thinking?"

I shook my head in puzzlement. "I can't imagine. Was Monk using Mary Lopes as a last ditch effort to portray Helen as a sex-obsessed 'slut'? If so, why didn't anyone at Child Protective Services—or County Counsel—challenge the wisdom of using a suspected child molester as a witness? And more importantly, why were Mary and her husband excluded as suspects in the case? As neighbors and—prior to John's conviction—babysitters, they certainly had access to Katherine."

"You're right, of course. If CPS truly believed that Katherine was a victim of sexual molestation, as her acting out might have indicated, it behooved them to investigate her contact with the Lopeses, one of whom is a suspected child molester and the other of whom is a true pervert." Judge Shriver then proceeded to briefly recount the Lopeses' own child molestation trial, over which he himself had presided.

"Actually," I corrected the judge, "the 'missing page' suggests that Bickel *did* investigate them. But he was so determined to prosecute Helen that he didn't follow up the obvious leads in Mary Lopes's statements. Instead, he covered them up and even recruited Mary to serve as a witness against Helen."

"Well, Bickel wasn't the only one who made mistakes," the judge offered.

"No," I replied. "That's just it. Maybe Bickel's ineptitude and deliberate interference could be excused as the products of an unstable person being thrust into a position for which he was ill-equipped, either intellectually or emotionally. But the fact that CPS and County Counsel let his machinations lead them astray was patently criminal."

"Careful," Judge Shriver cautioned, "When you use a word like 'criminal' you better have some incontrovertible evidence. The whole lot of them—I mean CPS, County Counsel, and the police—completely botched this case. But other than Bickel, I think they were well intentioned."

Personally, I wasn't so sure, but I kept this opinion to myself.

Soon the conversation turned to lighter subjects. Coincidentally, both of us had young daughters whose club soccer teams had vied for their regional youth soccer championship, but unfortunately lost. One big difference though, I took the loss much more personally and shared the girls' pain and disappointment much more deeply than did Judge Shriver.

On the drive home after our dinner it occurred to me that the same was true of the Cross case. Judge Shriver was already dispassionately filing away the Cross case in a neatly categorized hierarchy of cases won, cases lost, and cases botched. But I knew that I would always remember this case with a tinge of unresolved bitterness—the sour taste of injustice. Helen had won her case, but at what cost?

MOTHER-DAUGHTER INCEST AND THE LIMITS OF RATIONALITY

Steven D. Pinkerton & Paul R. Abramson

The main text of *A House Divided* tells an emotionally harrowing tale of a mother's fight to retain custody of her daughter amid horrifying accusations of incest. Helen Cross was accused of a heinous and unforgivable crime: sexually abusing her five-year-old daughter, Katherine. The evidence against Helen was weak at best, consisting of reports from an "expert" psychologist (Dr. Carrier), a pediatric gynecologist (Dr. Dworkin), the police, and Katherine's teachers. There was no physical evidence that Katherine had ever been sexually abused, although Dr. Dworkin testified that the findings from her examination of Katherine were "consistent" with molestation (they were also consistent with several alternative explanations). The suspicions of incest were magnified by Katherine's statements that "mommy does it to me at home," apparently referring to masturbatory acts. However, as Dr. Abramson established through a series of simple experiments, Katherine's intent had been misinterpreted. Nevertheless, the near-total lack of evidence of wrongdoing did not impede an overzealous prosecution, fueled by the prejudices and pathologies of a young social worker, Matt Bickel, who fed misinformation to several of the prosecution's witnesses in an effort to ensure Helen's conviction. Ultimately, it appears that Helen was guilty of nothing more than a misunderstanding concerning the application of Neosporin to her daughter's genital region.

The Cross case highlights several psychojudicial issues relevant to the assessment and prosecution of mother-daughter incest. The standard approach to assessing whether incest has occurred emphasizes the child's testimony, together with whatever corroborating physical and psychological evidence exists. However, as this case demonstrates, this approach can be extraordinarily problematic. Although some incest cases are relatively straightforward (especially when a confession is obtained), the contested and protracted cases are anything but simple. Complications and misinterpretations can arise at any of several junctures, including the child's comments, the police investigation, the investigation by the Child Protective Services, the psychological evaluation, the pediatric gynecological examination, and the litigation itself.

Although most cases of incest are not as convoluted as the one considered here, definitive evidence of abuse is seldom available, unless the perpetrator confesses. Moreover, often the evidence that is available is deeply flawed, as noted in the Cross case. As a result, the critical question of whether or not incest has indeed occurred can seldom be answered with certainty. And, even if it can, a conviction is not assured.

The question of when to litigate is dependent upon both the quality of the evidence and the probability of conviction. In this essay, we argue that it should also depend on two additional factors that are often overlooked in the zeal to prosecute suspected incest perpetrators: the base rate of the crime and the potential costs associated with bringing an innocent person to trial.

Mother-daughter incest appears to be comparatively rare (i.e., the base rate of mother-daughter incest is small). Therefore, in the absence of compelling evidence of abuse, most suspected instances of mother-daughter incest are likely to be red herrings. Second, we argue that decisions to litigate should also carefully consider the costs and benefits, to both parent and child, of pursuing a conviction. "False-positives"—that is, unwarranted incest charges against innocent parents—can have substantial psychological and emotional costs for parents and children alike. In some cases, litigation may not be worth it.

Thus, we will argue that "rational" concerns—about the likelihood that incest has occurred, the quality of evidence, the probability of conviction, and the potential costs and benefits of litigation—should guide the decision of whether to prosecute or not. We will then discuss some of the reasons why this rational approach to litigating incest cases is seldom followed, focusing on the desire to protect the child "at all costs," and the on limits of rationality in human decision making.

INCEST: DETECTION AND PROSECUTION

Incest litigation has a unique status within the law. Historically, incest was an underreported and underprosecuted crime. Until very recently, the notion that a parent could sexually abuse his or her own child was considered unfathomable, particularly by the better-educated classes. Incest accusations had little credibility and law enforcement officials were loath to arrest suspected perpetrators or to prosecute accordingly. Often, children who made their accusations public were shamed and ridiculed, and the threat of libel from alleged abusers was a serious concern (Abramson et al., 1997; Finkelhor, 1979).

However, once the true extent of incest—which is now recognized to occur across all social groups and professions—was fully appreciated, myriad social welfare and law enforcement agencies rallied to protect sexually abused children. Mandatory reporting laws were established and enforced, and the media began to accord this heinous crime the coverage it deserves.

Even more than other forms of childhood sexual victimization, incest involves extraordinarily complex issues that pit the rights of children to be protected from abuse, against the custody rights of their parents. Generally, the rights of children are subsumed under the rights of their parents or guardians. Parents make all critical decisions for their children in the areas of health, education, and religion. This is deemed necessary because children, based upon their emotional and intellectual immaturity, are presumed to be incapable of making reasonable, informed choices, and thus need their parents to function in a decision-making capacity on their behalf. Children are thereby disenfranchised for their own good.

Although this arrangement generally benefits children, it becomes a nightmare when their parents (or guardians) are sexual abusers. Incestuously abused children are effectively imprisoned by their parents. The familial environment ensures abusive parents regular access to their children for purposes of sexual exploitation. Because they control their children's physical and social environments, parents can easily hide this exploitation and can use the children's immaturity and lack of credibility as a shield against incrimination.

Though reticent to accuse their parents, incest victims are often frightened or traumatized enough to discuss the abuse with sympathetic professionals. Doctors, social workers, guidance counselors, teachers, psychologists, and so forth are now trained to be attentive to such cues and to approach instances of suspected incest with sensitivity, trust, and understanding. State laws require professionals to report all suspicions of incest, and the Department of Child Protective Services is empowered to investigate such accusations, creating a strong advocacy system for children who are sexually victimized by adults. In addition, most large police departments include special units composed of men and women who have received focused training in the investigation of childhood sexual abuse cases and the protection of children.

Are all of these safeguards necessary?

Absolutely! Children are among the most vulnerable members of our society. They are easily preyed upon and the crimes against them are particularly harmful and traumatic. This is especially true of incestuous abuse, where the abuser is also the ultimate authority (legal and otherwise) on the child's behalf. The greatest tragedy, of course, is that incestuously abused children require protection from the very persons ordinarily charged with protecting them from harm. Thus, extraordinary safeguards and sanctions are necessary—and must be vigilantly enforced—to protect children from incestuous abuse.

Such safeguards notwithstanding, parents also need protection against false accusations of incest. Though the harms of incest are well appreciated, the harmful consequences resulting from false accusations are also quite real, and can sometimes be devastating. Wrongly removing a child from the home and putting him or her in foster care with unknown adults can be traumatic for the parents and child alike. Extended separations from loving parents can engender adverse long-term psychological sequelae for the child, while for the parent, the emotional and psychological toll of enduring a long, drawn-out battle to demonstrate one's innocence can be immense, as Helen Cross reluctantly discovered.

Given the sizable costs associated with false accusations of incest, any such accusation should be supported by substantial evidence. Yet, the lack of conclusive evidence in the Cross case did not appreciably deter the prosecution. Why not?

THE TRIAL OF HELEN CROSS

In hindsight, the fact that Helen Cross was brought to trial appears an obvious legal travesty, defensible only by a desire to "protect the child at all costs." Many people, psychologists, social workers, and criminal prosecutors included, endorse this dictum as a cardinal rule in cases of suspected sexual abuse. While there are many legitimate reasons to follow this dictum, one may question whether the interests of the child are the only ones that should matter in such cases—particularly when investigating suspected mother-daughter incest.

Even if one adopts this limited perspective, it does not necessarily follow that the child's welfare is best served by prosecuting every mother suspected of abuse. Depending upon the degree of certainty, prosecution itself entails emotional costs for both the mother and child that could, in some instances, outweigh the perceived danger of leaving the child in the home, especially if the evidence is problematic. The Cross case is an excellent example of this very phenomenon.

The overriding concern in such cases is, of course, whether or not the mother has committed incest with her daughter. How can we determine this with certainty? Unfortunately, no single diagnostic tool can reliably and consistently answer this critical question. Definitive proof of incest is usually available only if the parent confesses, or if there is physical evidence of penetration (such as semen or a sexually transmitted pathogen), or a physical record of the crime, such as a photograph or videotape.

A confession resolves the question of whether incest actually occurred. Often, perpetrators confess only because they have gotten caught (or been detected) in their crime. Perpetrators may confess because they feel guilty, hope it will provide solace to their victims, or presume it will affect their sentencing. Sometimes, all three motives are involved.

Confessions also greatly help victims because they validate accusations, rally support, and enhance prosecutions. A confession is also perceived as evidence that the perpetrator is amenable to therapy. Although this makes intuitive sense, it is not necessarily consistent with the perpetrator's motivations for confessing. Receiving a reduced sentence, for example, is unrelated to the success of psychotherapy. Also, given the recidivism rate of sex offenders in general, it is unclear how effective treatment programs are for perpetrators of incest.

Besides a confession, there are two other types of evidence that unquestionably demonstrate that incest or sexual abuse has occurred. The first is when sexually explicit photographs (or pornography) of the victim and perpetrator are discovered. Such evidence clearly indicates that abuse took place, and if the perpetrator appears in the photographs, his or her complicity is easy to establish. The second kind of incontrovertible evidence is the presence of a sexually transmitted disease or other evidence of overt sexual activity in the child. When a six-year-old girl tests positive for gonorrhea, it is clear that she has been sexually abused. If the suspected perpetrator is infected with a similar strain, it becomes much easier to obtain a conviction, or possibly, to elicit a confession.

But what if there is no confession, pornography, or sexually transmitted disease in evidence? How can we determine if incest occurred, particularly mother-daughter incest, which is a relatively rare form of sexual abuse?

A BASE RATE ARGUMENT

Determining whether mother-daughter incest has occurred in a particular case is an exceedingly complex measurement issue that admits no easy solution. Psychologists, of course, often grapple with difficult-to-measure concepts, such as intelligence, extroversion, and neuroticism. Indeed, the measurement issues faced in psychology are sufficiently complex to merit a distinct subdiscipline of academic psychology devoted to this topic. Thus, many major universities offer a Ph.D. specialization in issues related to psychological measurement.

In 1955, Paul Meehl and Albert Rosen of the University of Minnesota published a study that is now recognized as a seminal work in the field of psychological measurement (Meehl & Rosen, 1955). In this article, the authors argued for the need to take into account the "base rate" (or prevalence) of a particular phenomenon when assessing the diagnostic accuracy of an instrument designed to measure that phenomenon. For example, imagine that we have constructed a simple questionnaire to detect pedophilia among adult men. For simplicity, we can assume that there are only two possible scores on the questionnaire: either the person appears to be pedophile (a "positive" test result) or he doesn't (a "negative" result). We define the *sensitivity* of a diagnostic test to be the probability that a true pedophile would receive a positive score. Conversely, the *specificity* of the test is the probability that a person who is not a pedophile would receive a negative score. Thus, a sensitive test is one that correctly identifies pedophiles, whereas a specific test is one that rarely misclassifies men who are not pedophiles.

Obviously, we'd like our diagnostic tests to be both highly sensitive and highly specific. Often, however, increases in sensitivity can be obtained only with concomitant decreases in specificity, and vice versa. For example, the most sensitive "test" would be to simply *assume* that every man is a pedophile. The sensitivity of this "test" is 100% because it correctly identifies every pedophilic man. However, it also produces a large number of "false-positives" because of its indiscriminate nature, hence it is not very specific. Conversely, a "test" that declares that no man is a pedophile has 100% specificity because it never incorrectly identifies anyone as being pedophilic when in fact he is not. But it misses all those men who actually are pedophiles ("false-negatives").

Notice, though, that the accuracy of the "assume-every-man-is-a-pedophile" test (or the "assume-no-man-is-a-pedophile" test) depends on the proportion of men who actually *are* pedophiles. In a population with a high "base rate" (or prevalence) of pedophilia, the "assume-every-man-is-a-pedophile" test would result in relatively few false-positives, whereas the same test would yield a substantial number of false-positives if applied to a population with a low base rate of pedophilia (Meehl & Rosen, 1955).

The same is true of psychological instruments with imperfect sensitivity and specificity: how well a test performs in a particular population critically depends upon the base rate of the phenomenon of interest. Below we introduce a simple mathematical framework to illustrate this point.

First, define the *accuracy* of a diagnostic test, relative to a given population, to be the ratio of the total number of correct diagnoses (i.e., true-positives and true-negatives) to the total number of people tested:

$$\text{Accuracy} = \frac{T^+ + T^-}{N},$$

where T^+ denotes the number of true-positives, T^- denotes the number of true-negatives, and N denotes the total number of people tested. In other words, the accuracy of a test is the proportion of people it correctly classifies (as pedophiles, for instance).

Both T^+ and T^- can be expressed in terms of the *sensitivity* and *specificity* of the test and the base rate of the phenomenon of interest (which we continue to assume is male pedophilia):

$$T^+ = N^* R^* \text{Sensitivity} \quad \& \quad T^- = N^*(1 - R)^* \text{Specificity},$$

where R is the population base rate (hence, $N^* R$ equals the number of pedophilic men). The equations for determining the number of false-positives and false-negatives parallel those for calculating the number of true-positives and true-negatives:

$$F^+=N^*(1-R)^*(1-\text{Specificity}) \;\&\; F^-=N^*R^*(1-\text{Sensitivity}).$$

In this simple arithemetic framework, the accuracy of a test can be reduced to a function of the sensitivity and specificity of the test and the population base rate:

$$\text{Accuracy} = \frac{T^+ + T^-}{N} = R^*\text{Sensitivity} + (1-R)^*\text{Specificity}.$$

For example, if one-quarter of the men living in a city with a population of 600,000 are pedophiles (i.e., the base rate is 25%), then a test with 90% sensitivity and 80% specificity will identify 135,000 true-positives (real pedophiles) and 360,000 true-negatives (men who are not pedophiles). The remaining 105,000 people will be misclassified, with 90,000 false-positives (men falsely labeled as pedophiles) and 15,000 false-negatives (men who are pedophiles but who are not classified as such). The overall accuracy of this test is therefore 82.5%.

In their seminal paper, Meehl and Rosen (1955) focused on the impact that population base rates have upon the accuracy of psychological tests. As they noted, the accuracy of the "assume-every-man-is-a-pedophile" test equals the base rate R, whereas the accuracy of the "assume-no-man-is-a-pedophile" test equals $1-R$. If the base rate of pedophilia is low, as it is in most adult male populations, then the "assume-no-man-is-a-pedophile" test is actually very accurate—that is, the results of this test are correct in a substantial proportion of cases. Indeed, we easily can see that an alternative test is more accurate than the "assume-no-man-is-a-pedophile" test if and only if:

$$R * \text{Sensitivity} + (1 - R) * \text{Specificity} > 1 - R.$$

Or equivalently:

$$\frac{1 - \text{Specificity}}{1 - \text{Specificity} + \text{Sensitivity}} < R,$$

where "Sensitivity" and "Specificity" refer to the alternative test (Meehl & Rosen, 1955; Pinkerton & Abramson, 1992).

When the base rate, R, is small, $1 - R$ is large and even very sensitive and specific tests will fail to satisfy the above inequality. For example, consider an alternative test whose sensitivity equals its specificity. For this test to exceed the accuracy of the "assume-no-man-is-a-pedophile" test would require that its sensitivity and specificity exceed $1 - R$, which is highly unlikely if the base rate is small (e.g., one-tenth of one percent). Thus, the most accurate "test" in such circumstances is likely to be the expedient solution of assuming that no man is a pedophile.

As discussed in the main text, mother-daughter incest is comparatively rare, in general, and exceedingly rare in the absence of maternal psychosis or emotional imbalance. A simple base rate argument therefore suggests the extreme implausibility of mother-daughter incest. Consequently, even a very sensitive and specific instrument to detect the occurrence of incest is likely to generate far more false-positives than true-positives—that is, the vast majority of instances of suspected mother-daughter incest incidents that it identifies will be mistakes.

What is the base rate of mother-daughter incest? It is difficult to say, but suppose it is one in a million (which would suggest that a substantial number of incestuous episodes occur each year). Then, to improve on the simple rule of "assume that mother-daughter incest did not occur" would require a test of exceedingly high sensitivity and specificity. Indeed, a test with perfect (100%) sensitivity would need to be 99.9999% sensitive in order to improve on the accuracy of the "assume-that-mother-daughter-incest-did-not-occur" rule.

In actuality, the instruments used by police, social workers, and others concerned with the detection and prosecution of incest offenders (including interviews, clinical evaluations, etc.) are neither especially sensitive nor especially specific. Thus, from a strictly arithmetic standpoint, accuracy would be maximized by discarding the traditional assessment techniques and instead relying on a simple rule: in the absence of extraordinary evidence to the contrary, assume that mother-daughter incest did *not* occur. Reliance on this simple rule would greatly reduce the incidence of false-positives, in which women are falsely accused of incest, and thereby reduce the burden such cases place on the judicial and social welfare systems.

Why, then, isn't this simple, cost-saving rule embraced? The answer, quite obviously, is that although this strategy would reduce the number of false-positives (or falsely ac-

cused women) nearly to zero, it would also virtually eliminate the detection of true-positives—that is, cases in which
mother-daughter incest really did occur. Because incest is a
heinous crime with potentially severe psychological consequences for the child, society has adopted an extremely
cautious stance with regard to the detection of possible instances of mother-daughter incest. Suspected offenders are
essentially "guilty, until proven innocent," in order to ensure
maximal protection for potential victims of mother-daughter
incest.

In short, the problem with basing decision rules on simple diagnostic efficiency measures (such as the accuracy of a
test) is that these measures do not adequately reflect society's
preferences for particular outcomes over others. What is
needed, instead, is a decision-making procedure that explicitly incorporates societal preferences, or "utilities," as they
are sometimes called. Utilitarianism provides a theoretical
basis for all such procedures.

UTILITARIANISM

The roots of utilitarianism can be traced back at least as far
as the noted Greek philosopher Epicurus (342–270 B.C.E.),
who taught that pleasure is the supreme good and the at-
tainment thereof is the ultimate goal of life (Inwood &
Gerson, 1994). According to Epicurus, people should (and
naturally do) seek out pleasurable experiences and avoid

painful ones. (Epicurus used the terms "pleasure" and "pain" in their broadest connotation, to encompass the pleasures and pains of the body, mind, and spirit.)

The English moral and legal philosopher Jeremy Bentham (1748–1832) expanded upon and codified this Epicurean notion in his famous *Greatest Happiness Principle*. According to Bentham's like-minded countryman, John Stuart Mill (1806–1873):

> Utility, or the Greatest Happiness Principle, holds that actions are right in proportion as they tend to promote happiness, wrong as they tend to produce the reverse of happiness. By happiness is intended pleasure, and the absence of pain; by unhappiness, pain, and the privation of pleasure. (Mill in Ryan, 1987, p. 278)

Thus, the Greatest Happiness Principle provides a standard by which actions can be judged: an action is deemed to be ethical or "right" only inasmuch as it tends to enhance the happiness of the community as a whole. Indeed, Bentham himself proposed an explicit procedure for "estimating the tendency of any act or event" to promote the general happiness:

> Sum up the numbers expressive of the degrees of good tendency, which the act has, with respect to each individual, in regard to whom the tendency of it is good upon the whole: do this again with respect to each individual, in regard to whom the tendency of it is bad upon the whole. Take the balance; which, if on the side of pleasure, will give the general good tendency of the act, with respect to the total num-

ber or community of individuals concerned; if on the side of
pain, the general evil tendency, with respect to the same
community. (Bentham in Ryan, 1987, p. 88)

Bentham believed that the purpose of laws is to "aug-
ment the total happiness of the community," but he also realized that punishment, the agency through which legal
compliance is enforced, is itself an evil. Therefore, "upon the
principle of utility . . . [punishment] ought only to be admitted in as far as it promises to exclude some greater evil"
(Bentham in Ryan, 1987, p. 97). In particular, Bentham held
that punishment should be withheld when, in the balance, it
appears "unprofitable"—that is:

Where, on the one hand, the nature of the offense, on the
other hand, that of the punishment, are, in the ordinary
state of things, such, that when compared together, the evil
of the latter will turn out to be greater than that of the former. (Bentham in Ryan, 1987, p. 101)

For instance, if greater harm would be done to Katherine
and Helen Cross by removing the daughter from her
mother's home, then the utilitarian principles enunciated by
Bentham would favor leaving the child in the home (where
psychotherapy, etc., could be implemented).

More generally, because the principal objective of child
welfare laws is the protection of children, alternatives to removal that also protect the child from the possibility of further abuse—if indeed abuse has occurred—should also be
entertained (especially if the evidence is problematic). Although it is easy to endorse the notion that a molesting

mother should be punished (particularly if she has confessed, or if pornographic pictures have been discovered), it is more difficult to rationalize this course of action when the evidence of sexual abuse is controvertible. In such instances, removing the daughter from her mother's home and (possibly) imprisoning the mother may be unnecessary, provided that the abuse (if any) has ceased and there are well-founded expectations that it will not resume in the future. Bentham believed punishment to be needless "where the purpose of putting an end to the practice [e.g., mother-daughter incest] may be attained at a cheaper rate" (Bentham in Ryan, 1987, pp. 102–103)—through mother-daughter counseling, for example.

In the past century, utilitarianism has found widespread application as a foundation for decision making in a diverse array of fields, including business, medicine, and public policy. The basis for these applications owes as much to the seventeenth-century mathematicians Blaise Pascal (1623–1662) and Pierre de Fermat (1601–1665), who first formalized the concept of expected value maximization, as to utilitarians such as Epicurus, Bentham, and Mill. Expected value theory has its roots in gambling, a favorite pastime of seventeenth-century aristocrats.

The expected value of a particular bet is simply the expected payoff, minus the amount bet. In other words, the expected value equals the average profit that would be realized if the gamble were repeated some very large number of times.

The expected payoff for a particular bet is easy to calculate, in theory at least. First, calculate the expected payoff for each possible outcome (e.g., each possible combination of dice or each possible poker hand) by multiplying the payoff for that outcome by the probability that the outcome would occur. Then, add up the expected payoffs for all possible outcomes to obtain the overall expected payoff of the bet.

For example, suppose that two dice are rolled and that you have bet $1 that, in some combination, the dice will total 4. If the payoff for a "1-3" combination (i.e., a "1" on one die and a "3" on the other) is $18 and the payoff for a "2-2" combination is $36, then the expected payoff is: (2/36 * $18) + (1/36 * $36) = $2, because the probability that a "1-3" combination would occur is 2/36 (there are two ways to make this combination) and the probability that the "2-2" combination would come up is only 1/36. The expected value of this bet, obtained by subtracting the original bet from the expected payoff, is thus: $2 − $1 = $1. This bet is a good one, because its expected value is positive; on average, you would win a dollar for every dollar bet. (This example is pure fantasy, of course. Unless you are a capable card counter or a highly skilled poker player, or you know some other loophole, you will not find any positive expected value bets in Las Vegas.) Notice the similarity of this method for calculating expected value to Bentham's procedure for estimating the tendency of an action to promote the general happiness. A bet with a positive expected value is analogous to an action with a "general good tendency."

Expected utility theory is an obvious generalization of expected value theory, as described above. The only difference is that in expected utility theory, dollars are replaced by some measure of the *utility* of the different outcomes. For example, instead of being paid $18 for a "1-3" dice combination, suppose you were paid 18 "happiness units," and likewise you received a payoff of 36 happiness units for a "2-2" combination. If the dice game cost 1 happiness unit to play, then the expected utility (expected payoff minus initial bet) would be 1 happiness unit.

Utilities encode people's preferences for particular outcomes, at either an individual or a societal level. Specifically, the utility (or number of happiness units) associated with a particular action or event is its value to a particular person, or to society at large. Different people may value different outcomes to a greater or lesser extent. For instance, the utility of a dollar is likely to be much greater to a poor person, who values the food he or she can buy with it, than to a wealthy person who regularly dines at gourmet restaurants.

Utilitarianism in its modern guise presupposes that people act to maximize their expected utility, or at least argues that they should. That is, when faced with a choice between multiple alternative actions (e.g., should I bet on the "15" in roulette or place all my money on the black?), people should select the option that maximizes the expected utility of their choice.

The available psychological evidence suggests that the utility maximization assumption oversimplifies the complexities of human decision making, and therefore one may question the validity of utilitarianism as a *descriptive* theory of human choice. However, the *prescriptive* power of this theory is obvious to everyone who, like Bentham, believes that right actions should serve to enhance the common welfare.

A UTILITARIAN FRAMEWORK FOR DECISION MAKING APPLIED TO MOTHER-DAUGHTER INCEST

Society's conservative stance toward mother-daughter incest reflects an implicit weighting of the negative consequences of incest that is sufficient to overwhelm the often small likelihood that mother-daughter incest had really occurred, and an implicit undervaluing of the costs associated with false-positives (equivalently, false accusations). In this section we describe a simple expected utility model for evaluating the possible outcomes of a diagnostic test and discuss some of the implications of this model of rational decision making.

As noted above, Meehl and Rosen (1955) presume that the best measure of a diagnostic test's performance is its accuracy—that is, the proportion of cases classified correctly. Under this assumption an error is an error, regardless of whether it is a false-positive or a false-negative. But in many circumstances, such as the detection of mother-daughter incest, avoiding one type of error is much more important than avoiding the other. Similarly, one type of "success" may be more important than another. Moreover, the values attached to errors and successes often differ substantially. For example, ensuring that actual cases of mother-daughter incest are correctly identified as such may be viewed as being more important than preventing innocent suspects from being unduly prosecuted.

In general, the different possible diagnostic outcomes (true-positive, true-negative, false-positive, false-negative) may be associated with very different costs and benefits. (Table 1 presents an interpretation of these outcomes within the sexual abuse context.) By incorporating costs and benefits in the decision-making process, better informed choices can be made between competing alternatives, such as the decision of whether to prosecute or not (Pinkerton & Abramson, 1992).

The basic notion behind the utilitarian approach to decision making is the assumption that accuracy is not always the best indicator of the value of a diagnostic test, especially when large differences exist between the costs of different decision categories. Instead, decision makers should strive to maximize utility (or "happiness" as Bentham referred to it), or equivalently, to minimize cost. What follows is a simple mathematical framework for conceptualizing such decisions.

Table 1: CORRESPONDENCE BETWEEN ANALYTIC FRAMEWORK AND SEXUAL ABUSE CASES

DIAGNOSTIC RESULT	ACTION/OUTCOME
True-positive	Trial of actual perpetrator
False-positive	Trial of innocent parent or caretaker
True-negative	No trial of innocent parent or caretaker
False-negative	No trial of actual perpetrator

Let λ_{F+} and λ_{F-} represent the costs associated with the two erroneous diagnoses (false-positive and false-negative, respectively), and let β_{T+} and β_{T-} denote the benefits associated with a correct diagnosis (true-positive or true-negative, respectively). (In this framework, benefits are viewed as negative costs, and vice versa.) Assume that the four diagnostic outcomes each occur with some probability P, as shown in Table 2 (for example, P_{T+} is the probability of obtaining a true-positive result). The probabilities obviously depend on the sensitivity and specificity of the test, as well as on the base rate of the phenomenon of interest. For example, the true-positive probability (P_{T+}) equals the product of the base rate and the sensitivity of the test (similar relationships hold for the other probabilities—see Table 2).

TABLE 2: SCHEMATIC OF UTILITIES AND PROBABILITIES ASSOCIATED WITH DIAGNOSTIC OUTCOMES

DIAGNOSTIC RESULT	BENEFIT OR COST	PROBABILITY
True-positive	B_{T+}	P_{T+} = Base rate* Sensitivity
True-negative	B_{T-}	P_{T-} = (1 − Base rate)* Specificity
False-positive	λ_{F+}	P_{F+} = (1 − Base rate)* (1 − Specificity)
False-negative	λ_{F-}	P_{F-} = Base rate* (1 − Sensitivity)

Suppose that we apply a diagnostic test to a population, classify people according to the results of this test, and take appropriate action (e.g., if the test suggests that this mother is a child abuser, then we will initiate procedures to prevent her from injuring her daughter or anyone else). The overall (net) benefit of applying the test-based decision rule to a given population is:

$$\text{Benefit} = [\beta_{T+} P_{T+} + \beta_{T-} P_{T-}] - [\lambda_{F+} P_{F+} + \lambda_F P_{F-}].$$

The first part of this equation concerns the benefits associated with correctly classified cases (true-positives and true-negatives), whereas the latter part corresponds to the costs associated with erroneously classified cases (false-positives and false-negatives).

As a society we should only implement and act upon the results of diagnostic tests whose benefits outweigh their costs—that is, whose net benefits are positive. Otherwise, the "general tendency" of such actions will be "evil." It is not clear, however, that society's actions always are consistent with this recommendation. The "tests" used to determine whether a potential incest case is worth pursuing in court, for instance, generally are not very sensitive or specific, and the base rate of incest (particularly mother-daughter incest) in most populations is extremely low. Combined, these characteristics conspire to generate large numbers of false-positive results, with attendant costs. The next section discusses some of these costs in greater detail.

PSYCHOLOGICAL AND OTHER COSTS

In order to protect children from ongoing sexual abuse, the primary objective of United States' social welfare apparatus and family court system is to ensure that false-negatives do not occur, because of the potentially immense psychological and emotional costs associated with leaving a child in an abusive environment. Although very few clinical cases of mother-daughter incest have been reported, the available evidence suggests that the long-term psychological sequelae experienced by survivors are similar to those seen in survivors of other forms of incest and in adults who were sexually abused as children. Psychoemotional disturbances may include clinical depression, anxiety, emotional isolation, self-destructive behavior, and low self-esteem. Survivors of parent-child incest may feel a deep sense of betrayal and have difficulty trusting others and forming close social relationships.

The feeling of betrayal is especially pronounced among women who were sexually abused by their mothers, because it constitutes a specific betrayal of the traditional role of mothers as protectors of their children. As a woman, a mother is also expected to identify with her daughter, with whom she shares a bond engendered by their shared femaleness. This expectation makes the abuse so much the worse. As one mother-daughter incest survivor explained, "Why would anybody's mom do that to them? She should know how I feel because she's a woman. She was once a little girl too" (Ogilvie & Daniluk, 1995).

Another common theme among survivors of this type of

abuse is that they (as children) must, in some way, have been responsible for their mothers' actions. The cultural belief that mothers do not sexually abuse their children is internalized by mother-daughter incest survivors, who may blame themselves for the abuse, leading to feelings of personal worthlessness and lowered self-esteem. Moreover, because mother-daughter incest is so rare, and therefore exceptional, survivors may feel greater shame and stigmatization than other adults who were sexually abused as children, because their abuse does not fit the social stereotype of male-female or male-male abuse (Ogilvie & Daniluk, 1995).

Many of these harms can be minimized by prompt detection of mother-daughter incest and removal of the child from the abusive environment or the institution of other measures to stop the abuse. Early identification and remedial action may be especially important for mother-daughter incest because the close proximity of parent and child provides opportunities for ongoing abuse. There are thus substantial (some might even say immeasurable) benefits to detecting cases of incest.

However, as demonstrated in the Cross case, the costs of falsely accusing and prosecuting a mother for incestuously abusing her daughter also can be grave (this corresponds to a false-positive in the above framework). These adverse consequences include psychological trauma to both mother and daughter, with perhaps enduring repercussions; destroying a family (Helen came very close to losing her daughter, permanently); discomfort associated with being subjected to repeated physical and mental assessments (including a gynecological exam for Katherine); the damage done to Helen's social reputation, which could be particularly acute in a small town such as Mendocino; potential social ostracism of the child; disruption of work, schooling, and other responsibilities; court costs, including the opportunity cost associated with diverting resources from the prosecution of an actual offender; and so forth.

Among the most significant of these costs, obviously, is the damage done to the mother-child relationship. Katherine was torn away from her mother and placed in foster care for several days before Helen regained temporary custody. Although she denied understanding the situation, Katherine was old enough to recognize the casual relationship between the information she had disclosed to the social workers and her removal from the home. She was thus aware that she had gotten her mother into trouble and that she was the cause of her own misfortunes. This must have caused intense feelings of guilt for Katherine, and possibly resentment for Helen.

In the future, of course, Helen would be much more reluctant to engage in any activity with her daughter that might be misconstrued as sexual in nature. Many normal mother-daughter interactions, such as bathing, dressing, and applying medication, require mothers to make intimate physical contact with their daughters' bodies, sometimes including their genitals. Helen had always been cautious about such contact—squeezing Neosporin over her daughter rather than applying it directly, for example—but after being tried as a child molester, she could not help but become even more wary.

Finally, what of the benefits of a true-positive (trying an actual perpetrator) or a true-negative (choosing not to bring an innocent person to trial)? Clearly, these are both highly desirable outcomes. Provided that the legal proceedings result in a conviction, the main benefit of pursuing criminal litigation against a sexual abuser is the possibility of removing the child from an abusive environment and protecting his or her psychological and emotional well-being. Some people might view the possibility of retribution and punishment as an additional benefit, while others might recast this as an opportunity to rehabilitate the offender. Conversely, the principal benefit of choosing not to try an innocent person lies in saving him or her from the pain and indignity of being put through the judicial wringer. Economically, the decision to forgo judicial proceedings might also save taxpayers a few dollars (indeed, there are economic consequences to all the possible outcomes listed in Table 1).

So, when should the prosecution of mother-daughter incest be pursued? The answer depends on the strength of the evidence for and against the possibility that abuse has actually occurred, the benefits and costs associated with the various outcomes of the decision to prosecute or not, and the likelihood that a conviction would be obtained if the case were brought to trial. In particular, the decision should take into account the sensitivity and specificity of the instruments (or techniques) used to assess likelihood of mother-daughter incest, and the base rate of mother-daughter incest in the community, as mediated by the probabilities of the different possible outcomes (true-positive, false-positive, true-negative, false-negative).

Recall, for example, that the probability of a false-positive equals $(1 - R)*(1 - \text{Specificity})$, where R is the base rate. Because the base rate for mother-daughter incest is so small (i.e., mother-daughter incest is so rare), the probability of obtaining a false-positive is essentially equal to the specificity of the techniques used to detect cases of incest. Given the limited specificity of the instruments designed to detect mother-daughter incest, such as psychological and gynecological examinations (assuming penetration has not occurred), and the opinions of teachers, caretakers, social workers, and other concerned individuals, we would therefore expect a large number of false-positives in cases of suspected mother-daughter incest. Certainly, a substantial number of women accused of sexual abuse are, in fact, innocent. This is largely so because society favors *sensitive* instruments over *specific* ones for the detection of childhood sexual abuse. We would rather charge an innocent person than let a guilty one go free.

A very high false-positive rate is simply one of the prices we pay, as a society, for this approach to detecting potential cases of mother-daughter incest. To illustrate, assume that the base rate of mother-daughter incest is one in a million (which seems a reasonable, but probably high, estimate) and assume (arbitrarily) that incest-detection techniques are 90% sensitive but only 60% specific. From the specified base rate, we would expect that of 10 million women investigated for allegedly molesting their daughters, 10 would be actual perpetrators. The incest test, however, would identify a total of 4,000,005 women as abusers, 99.999% (all but 9) of whom actually would be innocent.

Because the likelihood of obtaining a false-positive is so high, or more accurately, the proportion of positives that are false-positives is so high, the aggregate cost associated with false-positive results (i.e., unfounded accusations of incest) is immense. Indeed, it is likely that these costs are sufficiently great to overwhelm the benefits of detecting the rare case of mother-daughter incest (remember that each false-positive result severely and adversely impacts the lives of both mother and daughter). Thus, from a purely rationalistic perspective, it might make sense to follow the simple "assume-mother-daughter-incest-did-not-occur" rule. Adopting this rule would improve the diagnostic accuracy of incest-detection techniques, while simultaneously minimizing the social costs associated with false prosecutions for mother-daughter incest. But is this an acceptable solution?

THE QUESTION OF PERSPECTIVE

Perhaps, in examining the question of when it is appropriate to prosecute, we must draw back from the utilitarian framework, in which a societal perspective is implicity assumed, and instead consider the competing perspectives of the various parties involved in a case such as Helen Cross's. The costs and benefits of bringing this case to trial are very different, depending on whose perspective we focus on. What does Child Protective Services stand to gain/lose if the case goes to trial? What about County Counsel? Other involved parties? When we consider such questions, it quickly becomes clear that the societal perspective is subservient to the competing, and often political agendas of these and other or-

ganizations, and the personal interests of individuals such as
Matt Bickel. For example, County Counsel must determine
whether the case is worth pursuing based on the likelihood
of successful prosecution and the gains that such would en-
tail (taking into account the possibility of confession), versus
the costs associated with losing the case, as well as those in-
curred simply by bringing the case to trial, regardless of the
outcome. On the other hand, Child Protective Services' mandate is to protect and advocate for potentially abused children.

With regard to the strength of evidence, the availability
of a plausible alternative theory for the events that Katherine
described (namely, Neosporin rather than a dildo) should
have substantially reduced the confidence placed in the incest theory. Bickel's insistent pursuit of the case and his
persistent dissemination of disinformation to all parties, appears to be the main reason why this plausible alternative
explanation was not given the credence it deserved. Bickel
was determined to see Helen lose custody of her daughter
and he was more than willing to bend the truth in his quest
for "justice." He convinced the defense's psychology expert,
Dr. Carrier, that Helen had refused to be evaluated and had
refused to provide the authorities with access to Katherine's
therapist. He also intimated to Dr. Carrier (and possibly to
the gynecologist, Dr. Dworkin, as well) that objects had been
inserted into Katherine's vagina. Moreover, he suggested that
Helen had been aware of Katherine's ongoing sexual behavior problems but had failed to take action, when in fact it
was Helen who had first brought these problems to the attention of the authorities, in addition to placing her daughter in therapy. No doubt Bickel had succeeded in persuading

his supervisor at Child Protective Services, Marcia Osborn, of the validity of these accusations. Thus, the disinformation spread throughout the nexus of concerned parties, eventually finding its way into multiple reports and other documents.

The confidence placed in the misinformation spread by Bickel was magnified by the "multiplicity of evidential sources" phenomenon, in which convergent testimony from multiple sources increases the credibility of received information. Most people, for instance, would be more confident in their favorite television weatherperson's forecast of snow if this forecast was confirmed by several other news programs. This reaction to obtaining confirmatory evidence is logical and rational, provided that the forecasts are indeed independent sources of information. But, what if it turned out that the different weather teams all relied on the same source of information (such as the National Weather Service), so that their forecasts were simply the same information delivered by multiple messengers? In this case, no more confidence should be placed in the several weather reports, taken in aggregate, than should be afforded any single report. Most of the damaging "evidence" against Helen originated from Bickel. But it gained credence as it was disseminated to other parties and repeated.

THE LIMITS OF RATIONALITY

What are the limits of rationality in this setting? First, it is clear that the societal perspective is often secondary to other concerns in real-world decision making, which often involves multiple actors with competing objectives, including political and personal agendas. The diffuse, fragmented nature of typical decision-making processes—where, for example, the attorney general advises County Counsel to try a case they cannot win—permits these sometimes parochial objectives to take precedence over more global, societal concerns. Thus, the actions that are taken, though detrimental to society as a whole, may or may not be beneficial to anyone in particular.

Clearly incest evokes a primitive distaste—perhaps innate—that is reflected in the incest taboos observed in all human cultures, as well as in the social arrangements that prevent incest within a wide variety of different animal species. But a careful consideration of the costs involved suggests that society's abhorrence of mother-daughter incest may, in fact, be disproportionate to its ultimate costs. As a result, the utilitarian cost-benefit framework fails to provide an adequate descriptive account of the continued fervor with which mother-daughter incest cases are pursued.

Because of the extreme harm that can result from incest, and our natural revulsion to all forms of childhood sexual abuse, incest may inhabit a region of human experience in which rationality is permitted no quarter, or limited standing at best. Several years ago, Amitai Etzioni (1988) proposed a novel alternative to the rationalistic/utilitarian model of decision making that might be applicable to this domain. In Etzioni's decision-making framework, most choices are made on the basis of emotional involvements and value commitments—so-called "normative-affective factors." These normative-affective factors, which include such normative values as justice and respect for personal autonomy, as well as emotional influences such as sympathy and love, "shape to a significant extent decision making, to the extent it takes place, the information gathered, the ways it is processed, the inferences that are drawn, the options that are being considered, and those that are finally chosen" (Etzioni, 1988).

According to Etzioni's theory, normative-affective factors define three distinct regions within the decision-making universe. In the first region, decisions are made solely on the basis of normative-affective factors. For example, for most of us there can be no choice between abusing a child or not—the latter is simply unconscionable; that is, it is ruled out by normative values that proscribe child abuse. Likewise, few of us could eat the flesh of our loved ones, even if required to ensure our personal survival (for example, after a plane crash in the Sierra Nevadas). In instances such as these, normative-affective considerations trump logical or rational ones. The second type of region are the "indifference" regions in which the absence of strong normative-affective preferences permits the decision maker to rely on logical-rational considerations to a greater or lesser extent.

In the final region of decision-making space, normative-affective factors infuse deliberations in such a way that logical-rational considerations play a relatively minor or secondary role to normative-affective concerns. Normative-affective factors may influence decision making by loading or coloring various facts, interpretations, and inferences, thereby shifting the balance away from a rational weighting of all relevant facts and toward a decision procedure in which certain factors take undo precedence. We propose that many decisions in sexual abuse cases inhabit this region of decision-making space.

Decisions regarding suspected cases of incest may admit only limited rationality, the crime itself being so heinous as to block out most other evidential or rationalistic factors. Moreover, once a suspect has been identified and one or more persons (such as Bickel and his colleagues at Child Protective Services) have convinced themselves of the suspect's guilt, then the horrors of incest color all subsequent deliberations and decisions. Perhaps this is why important evidence was overlooked in the Cross case and why obvious suspects such as the Lopeses were not pursued. The actors in this little drama concluded early on that Helen was guilty, and with this premature conclusion, rationality was abandoned.

REFERENCES

Abramson, P. R., Cloud, M. Y., Keese, R., & Girardi, J. (1977). Proof positive: Pornography in a day care center. *Sexual Abuse: A Journal of Research and Treatment, 9,* 75–86.

Etzioni, A. (1988). Normative-affective factors: Toward a new decision-making model. *Journal of Economic Psychology, 9,* 125–150.

Inwood, B. & Gerson, L. P. (Translators) (1994). *The Epicurus Reader.* Cambridge, MA: Hackett Publishing.

Finkelhor, D. (1979). *Sexually Victimized Children.* New York: Free Press.

Meehl, P. E. & Rosen, A. (1955). Antecedent probability and the efficiency of psychometric signs, patterns, or cutting scores. *Psychological Bulletin, 52,* 194–216.

Ogilvie, B. & Daniluk, J. (1995). Common themes in the experiences of mother-daughter incest survivors: Implications for counseling. *Journal of Counseling & Development, 73,* 598–602.

Pinkerton, S. D. & Abramson, P. R. (1992). Base rates revisited: Assessment strategies for HIV/AIDS. *Journal of Sex Research, 29,* 407–424.

Ryan A. (Editor) (1987). *John Stuart Mill and Jeremy Bentham: Utilitarianism and Other Essays.* New York: Penguin Books.